Praise for *The Life Organizer*

"As a busy creative entrepreneur and mom, I find it tempting to be run by my to-do list. If I'm not careful, I wind up feeling stressed — and I don't get to fully enjoy the process of all that I'm doing. Seeing *The Life Organizer* on my desk gently reminds me there is another way, a way to live with joy and productivity. I love this book!"

— Karen Salmansohn, bestselling author of *Prince Harming Syndrome*

"I've been a fan of Jennifer's work since her first book, and she never disappoints! *The Life Organizer* is not only smart and practical, it's compassionate and soulful — something most books on organization lack. This work takes mindful living to a whole new level and teaches concepts in a delicious and palatable way. Buy it, highlight it, get it messy. Watch your lovely life grow."

— Susan Hyatt, master life coach and author of *Create Your Own Luck*

"This wonderful book is a tribute to the sacred and very practical aspects of time management. If you want a more soulful, clear life, follow Jennifer Louden's advice."

— Judith Orloff, MD, author of *Positive Energy*

"You are not holding a book in your hands. Instead, imagine a set of sacred nesting dolls that you open, one by one, each delighting you more than the last. As you get to the precious one in the center, you find your own heart. It whispers, 'welcome home.'"

— Dawna Markova, author of *Spot of Grace* and cocreator of *Random Acts of Kindness*

Other books by Jennifer Louden

The Woman's Comfort Book
The Couple's Comfort Book
The Pregnant Woman's Comfort Book
The Woman's Retreat Book
Comfort Secrets for Busy Women

The Life Organizer

A Woman's Guide to a Mindful Year

JENNIFER LOUDEN

New World Library
Novato, California

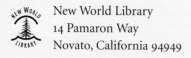

New World Library
14 Pamaron Way
Novato, California 94949

Illustrations by Alicia La Chance
Text design and typography by Tracy Cunningham

Library of Congress Cataloging-in-Publication Data
Louden, Jennifer.
The life organizer : a woman's guide to a mindful year / Jennifer Louden.
   p.   cm.
ISBN 978-1-57731-554-4 (hardcover. : alk. paper)
1. Women—Conduct of life. 2. Women—Psychology. 3. Goal (Psychology).
4. Self-realization in women. 5. Self-help techniques. I. Title.
HQ1221.L747 2007
158.1082—dc22   2006025422

First paperback edition, January 2014
ISBN 978-1-60868-245-4
Printed in China

New World Library is proud to be a Gold Certified Environmentally Responsible Publisher. Publisher certification awarded by Green Press Initiative.
www.greenpressinitiative.org

10 9 8 7 6 5 4 3 2 1

Contents

— ∞ —

Welcome

— ∞ —

*T*his book is my attempt to name, and give a form to, one way of living that I see emerging. It's a way of living in tune with what is, aware you always have a choice in how you react and what thoughts you believe; it's a way of living where paying attention to your inner knowing and intuition is as important as logic and to-do lists; it's a way of navigating life that embraces imperfection while heeding your true desires, where enoughness is your benchmark, and delight and savoring thread through it all. Most of all, it's a way of living rarely more than a breath away from astonishment at the marvel of simply being alive.

This is not a typical self-help book — it's not meant to be read cover to cover, it's not offering you advice, and it doesn't contain a single idea about how to make yourself better than or different from how you already are. Rather, it's an interactive guidebook, a collection of possibilities to inspire you in creating your way of participating with life and with your gifts. It invites you to use it in any number of ways, toggling between sections, creating your own Life Planner to record responses, depending on what you need or what you are curious about in the instance.

Having said that, here are some suggestions for possible ways to read the book, in case you're not sure where to dive in:

- Start with the Mood Shifter (p. 60) to find mindful questions, life-organizing tips, or stories that address the mood or situation you're in.

- Follow the questions in the Life Planner pages in order, recording your responses in your own Life Planner notebook.

- Open the Life Planner at random and choose a question or two that beguile you, irk you, or feel just right. Explore your responses using the five steps (pp. 8–9).

- Start with the Shape of Life Check-in (p. 224; all or any part of it), especially when you are feeling out of touch with yourself or haven't been life organizing for a while.

- Use one or all of the life-organizing steps (pp. 8–9) and the daily questions (pp. 26–28) and weave their insights throughout your daily life, especially when you are feeling off center, unsure, or in need of guidance.

- Visit jenniferlouden.com/lifeorganizer for more support, including an app, printable question pages, audios, and videos.

My prayer is that you will take the ideas and questions and stories I've collected here and create a life you love. I hope that this book will help you reduce stress, widen your perspective, take better care of yourself, manage your multiple roles, and let go of what you can't control — and that it will help you live in the sweet spot of self-compassion and action.

This is a book that *you* will finish by making the process your own. Then perhaps you will share what you have learned on Facebook at facebook.com/jenlouden.writer. Be sure to download all the free support at jenniferlouden.com/lifeorganizer. I host Life Organizer live events often to help you stay connected with yourself and other wise women. Join us please.

What Is Life Organizing?

W hat if there was a way to organize and guide your life that more closely resembled lying back on an inner tube as the current carried you along (with you occasionally adjusting your course because you want to smell a wild rose onshore or because you hit a bumpy stretch) rather than a furious, exhausting upstream paddle? What if self-mercy and listening to your authentic desires were your truest guides, far more trustworthy than gauging how much you accomplish in a day or what you earn? What if feeling confusion and uncertainty was actually a sign that you were on the right path? What if you could erase your sense of never having enough time or energy by cultivating a constant loving connection to yourself?

I have been focusing on just these questions, both personally and professionally, for more than twenty years. In general I noticed that most people seem to approach the process of organizing (whether a day, a project, or a life) by setting a goal, breaking it down into doable steps, and then staying the course until reaching the bull's-eye.

This method can be very effective in certain situations — I'm not suggesting that you abandon it — but it's only half the story, and we're starving for the rest, for a heart-based, spiritually informed, trusting story. We want to make room for, must make room for, chaos and interruption and accept that most of the time we don't know the big picture and we can only discern what to do one step at a time. This way of improvising our lives is built on our knowledge that we are creating our lives through how we think, how we react, and where we put our attention. We find that the most direct means to create a life that fits us is to embrace each moment as it arises.

I wrote this book because I want to develop this alternative way to shape a life and because it is one way to bring down the Berlin Wall of busyness, the ever-growing belief that to be successful, we must do more and do it faster, a story that is literally killing us. Be warned: this is a subversive way of looking at time. Once you embrace it, you can't go back. The old models will never wholly fit or satisfy you again; they will always be too much about willpower and force, about your private agendas and the mind's endlessly inventive stories.

The way I'm proposing in this book is frightening at first. It asks you, over and over, to trust, to loosen your grip on life, to soften with compassion and love toward yourself and others. It asks you to stop and feel, to tune in to what you really want and what you already know. To act with more boldness on your hunches and your values and to track with more clarity the outcomes of those bold actions. To serve all of life. This process is infinitely rich and it requires trust in your own experiences, in your own lived knowledge. "Test every-thing; hold fast to what is good" (1 Thess. 5:21) may become one of your mottoes, as might "But all shall be well, and all shall be well and all manner of things will be well," as Dame Julian of Norwich said.

Why is this approach toward creating our lives emerging now? I think it is because of the generation of women who were children in the 1970s and 1980s and watched their parents wear themselves out for a paycheck and are realizing they don't want to live the same way; because we're making spirituality part of our daily lives rather than something we do only on Sunday or on the meditation cushion; be-cause we are honoring intuition and other ways of knowing; and because we've reached the boiling point. We can't live in perpetual exhaustion any longer. We realize that our modern lives aren't totally working, personally or for the planet, so we ask ourselves, What can we create to help us survive and thrive?

Whatever the reasons, more and more women (and some men) are rejecting the overstriving, forcing, rushing, making-life-happen mode and developing a more intuitive yet grounded way to discern and sort the choices available to us. On the surface, it doesn't always look that different, but inside, it feels like the difference between a business suit and organic cotton pj's. I believe, with my whole body, that it is part of the change so many of us are already making or are yearning to make, and yet we have little idea how to talk about it, how to build on it, and how to make it *practical*. Here's how three women who have been using some of these principles and ideas have described it:

Poppy: "It's about living with greater awareness, cherishing yourself, and finding balance so as to be the most 'you' version of yourself that you can be. It's about becoming."

Wendy: "It's about honor, in several senses of the word: 1) Honor (as in respect) for ourselves, our needs, our bodies, our desires, our wishes. 2) Honor (as in truthfulness and integrity) about ourselves, our needs, our desires and wishes — whether they are 'good' or 'bad' — and in our behavior with others. 3) Honor (as in recognition and reverence) for the goodness and power within us, for the world's goodness and power, and for the Great Divine Entity (whatever you want to call him/her/it/them)."

Helga: "For me, it is about my search for sustained happiness. Aspects include feeling pleased, content, glad, satisfied, and comfortable. It's being happy with myself and what I have in my life. I'm on a journey toward resting comfortably within myself, in the sense of being my own safe place or refuge while staying interconnected with all living things. It takes me to the basics I need for the journey. To be consistently happy I need to know who I am (all parts of me, with no judgment); what I want (body, mind/spirit, heart); how I can be who I am (peacefully); and how I can have what I want (without doing harm).

"Life organizing is also about supplying the questions that get me there a bit faster. And, since the journey does not have an end, life organizing accompanies my twists and turns to always get me back to the source and to what really counts."

"Trust the Life Process"

There is a caveat: this new way of creating our lives can get derailed if we connect it to balance, as in, "If I could just figure out how to balance all these parts of my life, all these demands on my time, and all these interests, I'd be okay." When we're in this frame of mind, we'll always be searching, often more and more desperately, for the holy grail of balance; *but we're never going to find it with the eyes or the tools we're using.* Balance becomes a girdle, a rigid form into which we try to squeeze ourselves so that our lives will (finally!) be the perfect shape and we will (finally!) be right, safe, and on top of things. Yet this notion of balance is a false ideal that moves us further away from wholeness and ourselves. Real balance comes only when we are in loving touch with ourselves.

The new framework that we are hungering for is what I call "life organizing." I've spent the past thirteen years observing and articulating tools we can use to create humane lives that we love. These tools have emerged out of my work with thousands of women and from observing what friends, mentors, and prominent women in our culture are forging. My search led me first to design a new kind of date book, then to write my last book, *Comfort Secrets for Busy Women*, and finally morphed into an engagement calendar and an Internet forum. In truth, I kept trying to let the damn project go. Hadn't I done enough with it? Women were reporting good results. Why couldn't I leave well enough alone? But I knew there was more to be articulated about this new way of being that I saw so many of us trying so hard, sometimes so desperately, to master. Finally I outlined its principles as follows:

- A heart-centered intuitive way to shape our lives by listening to the still, small voice inside, by seeing life as the supreme creative act, a wild ride of choosing, improvising, and trusting our desires.

- An ability to live from the belief — at least some of the time — that we are beloved and that there are forces much larger than us to be rested upon.

- A way to use all that we've learned to sort through and choose from the many options and interests that can overwhelm us daily.

- A map, created over time, of our gifts so that we can clearly see, honor, and offer these gifts to the world.

- The remembrance that we know enough now to have a life that works — we just forget or doubt it or let our wisdom be buried under demands and erroneous stories of what life should look like. Or as Lain Ehmann, writer, business owner, and mother of three, said, "I don't need someone else's solutions; what I need is a *process for finding my own solutions.*"

- A way of planning our days that takes into account the true form and flow of a woman's life — rarely linear, always forged in connection, deeply influenced by our bodies, intimate with the often-difficult dance between what we want and what our life requires of us.

- Above all, a capacity to be guided by self-kindness and the unfolding beauty of life actually experienced.

When to Do It

When you awaken
When you are ready for bed
When you need to make a choice
When you are stuck, bored, depressed, or as flat as
    stale pita bread
When what you "have to do" feels hard, heavy, or
    plain impossible
When everyone wants a piece of you
When you want to help or serve others
When you are sure there is no way forward or no way to
    create what you want
When you want to bring something new into being
When you feel everything is up to you
When you are yearning for connection

Though I knew on a deep level that this is what we all yearn for, after writing a rotten first draft and a better but still hazy second draft, I wasn't getting much closer to articulating how to get it. I simply couldn't pin down all that I wanted to convey, the grace that permeates life when we actively surrender. Then these words from *The Biology of Transcendence* by Joseph Chilton Pearce leapt off the page and sent chills up my arms: "Transcendence, the ability to rise, and go beyond limitation and restraint, is our biological birthright, built into us genetically and blocked by enculturation.... Once we have been faithful in small works by which we learn to trust the life process, larger and larger works become possible." I then clearly saw that I wanted this book to champion the evolution of applying our spiritual understanding and our values to choosing and shaping a life you love — a life that shines because it fits you, a life that is, by its very nature, balanced because it is aligned with what you most treasure and enjoy. A life that matches your insides, a life guided by something larger than you and yet always chosen by you.

Yes, it is possible.

But What Is It *Really*?

The life-organizing process consists of — and of so much more than — five steps you can use when planning your week or your day or your few moments. They are:

1. Connect: Moving your energy is the gateway to wisdom, a great place to start.

2. Feel: Tuning in to your heart, which knows what your next step is, gives you information that your head can't.

3. Inquire: Asking a mindful question opens up possibilities you literally couldn't see before.

4. Allow: Opening to your next step — allowing love, inspiration, and knowing to come into your body and heart — informs and directs you in this new way.

5. Apply: "How we spend our days is how we spend our lives," writer Annie Dillard once observed. Without action, without decision, you remain in possibility, which is safe and beautiful but eventually enervating and boring.

> Whenever we codify anything, our minds like to get all persnickety about the "right" way to do it, and our attention gets stuck on that instead of on our actual experience. Don't focus on the five steps or the Life Planner — focus on your experiences.

It is also — and it is more than — a physical planner you design that encourages you to discern and track your spiral of growth, your choices, and your gifts using the five steps, as well as six additional concepts we'll get to in a bit. Why do I say "and it is more than"? Because I want to be very clear that this isn't the only way to live from the inside out. That would be absurd! That's the key characteristic of life organizing — it is always evolving, and it is unique to you.

We are making it up as we go along — and this is crucial to remember, *because it will feel like that, and that's perfectly normal.* This is fluid and flexible improvisation, and more often we know it by *what it is not* rather than by what it is. It's as if we were sketching in the faint outlines of a barely perceived possibility or layering rich

A rule

A should

A program

Something that must be done
every day or done to make
you good or right

Elaborate or time-consuming

About believing anything

pigments, step-by-step, to create a vivid reality-in-the-making. We are consciously participating in shaping the unique work of art that is our lives, and as with all works of art, there are a bizillion ways we could go. My attempt to distill what we are experiencing into five steps and a planner will hopefully never become a "should" but rather will be a recognition: "Oh, that's what I've been doing" or "That's the extra piece I need to put this way of relating to my life together." Another important characteristic of life organizing is that — as with all spiritual practices — it works best when it is woven into daily life. It helps you remember that choice happens in every moment; the most brilliant artist is sustained in her art by daily practices that help her keep following her gut.

When you start to embrace life organizing, you will be:

- Saving time and energy by accessing greater sources of knowing than your conscious mind.

- Increasing your creativity and energy by accepting and embracing your quirky, dented, perfectly imperfect individual self.

- Seeing yourself as the creator of your life instead of as a victim; focusing on what you want to bring into being instead of on the problems you need to solve.

- Trusting and investigating your desires, engaging with them as a way to identify your gifts and contributions to the world.

- Discovering a whole new way to approach questions like "Should I eat this?" or "Is this wasting time?"

- Honing your ability to accept what is happening now, without cluttering the moment with the past or future or with judgments.

- Finding and living your life, instead of someone else's (the biggest time and energy saver of all!).

Getting Started

You organize your life both in the moment and when you need a longer viewpoint — of your day or your week or your month. The process of gaining a longer viewpoint is similar to sitting down with your calendar or day planner, and in fact, many women work with their Life Planners alongside their traditional calendars. Life organizing in the moment brings the big picture into the now and works in many situations — from helping you choose what to do next, to reducing stress, to helping you live your values. Use the five steps to lead you into the process until you make it your own. Together, these methods will help you create a flexible, heart-guided, and self-loving structure for composing a life you are proud to call yours.

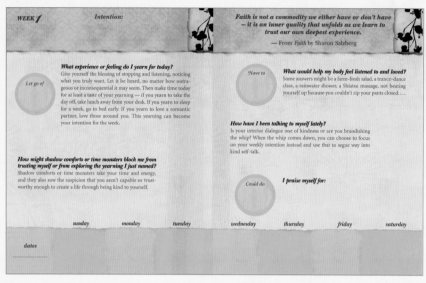

Below I provide descriptions of several different ways to get started on life organizing, including the time you'll need for each.

Life Organizing in the Moment

It's midmorning, and several minor crises have derailed you. Your plan for the day is in shambles, your to-do list feels like a boulder around your neck, and all you want to do is hide. You're reaching for a Diet Coke in the hopes that it will give you the energy to decide which item on your list to tackle and that it will change your frazzled mood. Then you remember that there's another way. You feel your feet connecting with the ground beneath you. You take a deep breath and reach your arms overhead, exhaling with a huge sigh. You put your hand on your heart and recall feeling loved when hanging out with a dear friend yesterday. Hand on heart, you gently ask, "What choice feels the easiest in this moment?" You take a breath. Perhaps a brief image of your friend comes to mind. Or maybe you hear a refrain from an old song, and when you focus on it, you realize it reminds you of your friend.

Time needed: One minute, or as long as it takes to get a soda out of the fridge, open it, sip.

> Try life organizing while on the treadmill, walking, biking, even sweeping the floor. Repetitive physical action can calm the monkey mind and can help you hear more clearly.

Using the Life Planner

It's Sunday night, and you're thinking about your upcoming week. You pour yourself your favorite soothing drink, grab your Life Planner, and curl up on the couch. You review your last few responses — they may take the form of notes, doodles, or even collages — and you remember that you didn't check in last week. It suddenly makes sense that you've been feeling a little off, tenser than usual. You flip to the next "month" of questions, read over them, and then take a moment to close your eyes and connect with your idea of Spirit or nature or relaxation. After a few moments, you feel drawn to lying on the floor to

> ### *What Life Organizing Is*
>
> Coming into the present
> Asking for guidance, help, support
> Listening, receiving, opening
> Applying, taking the next step
> Seeing if the path you are taking
> > fits you, feels right,
> > and aligns with your values
> A structure for learning from
> > your inner experience

stretch. You find yourself doing a few cat/cow stretches and tensing and relaxing your face. You spy a favorite poetry book that's fallen under the couch, pull it out, and read a poem. Now you feel ready to consider the questions and to write a few phrases in your notebook in response. Yet after doing one month of questions, you still feel unsure about the coming week, so you flip through the Life Planner until you find two more questions that help you hear what you need to know — for now. You make a few more notes and then spend a moment resting, hand on heart, asking if there is anything else you need to know. You end with a thank-you to yourself.

Time needed: ten to twenty minutes.

It is not how you do each step or the sequence in which you do them that matters. What does matter is that you hold the intention *to approach life organizing, to approach the whole of your life, by honoring yourself just as you are in this moment* and by being curious about what you feel drawn to do, or not do, next. This is not a step-by-step plan for living in perfect flow — that would be perfection masquerading as spiritual wisdom, another way to grasp after enlightenment — but rather a series of instructions to help you loosen the grip, enjoy yourself more while tending your multiple interests and connections. Encourage a mood of compassion and curiosity, knowing there is no one way and rarely one right answer, and you will find exactly what you need.

Using the Five Steps

Let's explore the five steps, an integral part of life organizing, in more depth.

Step 1: Connect

You are full of energy — literally. Tests such as the EEG, EKG, PET, and MRI all offer various visions of that energy. Your brain works by electrochemically connecting neurons. Your nerves use energy-triggering muscle fibers to move. Beyond these measurable energies, there are subtler energies that wisdom traditions have acknowledged for thousands of years — like chi or *prana*, two different ways of saying life force. You experience these subtle energies all the time — when someone stands too close to you and you back up, or when you sense that someone is looking at you. The most dramatic ex-ample is when you are with a person or animal at the time of their death. One moment you feel their life force, and the next you don't.

The first element of life organizing is to acknowledge and engage with this subtle energy, the life force that is always present. You don't have to do anything new. You already *know* how to do this. Potter, dancer, and ecologist Paulus Berensohn stated it beautifully in a radio interview: "Movement is the law of life. When there's no movement, there's no life. Song and dance are the laws of the universe, vibration and momentum are part of life, and you don't have to do the tango to be a dancer, to dance is to know that we have this animal body." Right now, if you wish to, notice what your body most feels like doing to enliven its energy. Maybe it's stretching your arms over your head while taking in a deep breath, massaging your head and temples, or sensing how gravity is supporting you in this moment. How would your body like to open right now? By recognizing that you are a being made up of energy and by inviting that energy to wake up, you open the door to the temple of *you*.

> If you aren't sure about what comes to you, ask your heart, "Is that accurate?" Breathe, and wait for a signal from your heart. If your heart says no, ask, "What do I need to hear? What would fit me better?" You may find yourself going back and forth several times to refine the guidance or ideas or impressions you receive.

Bringing your body into this process can be as basic as reminding yourself that you *have* a body. This is often easier said than done; it can be challenging, especially in the midst of a stressful day or week, to stop and check in with your body, your energy. Your mind may tell you that there is no time to get a drink of water and breathe, to pause and stretch, let alone to go outside and feel the breeze on your skin. (I once heard a woman say that she put off going to the bathroom for so long that she had to pee in the bushes at her front door because she couldn't wait to unlock the front door.) Your mind means well — it wants to get things done and stay on top of things — but if you leave it in charge, you will completely burn out because your mind can go faster and farther than your body will ever be able to. For example, my mind can write a book in fifteen seconds, while my body is still enjoying a hot shower.

You might become grateful for the smell of the tea you're about to pour hot water over. You might become aware of the warmth of a smile someone is offering you. You might roll your neck or your shoulders a few times. You might notice the texture of the shirt you are wearing. Simple. Always available.

Questions to Consider

The purpose of these questions is to help you notice what the most natural and easiest ways are for you to listen to your body, especially when you want to life organize. Jot down a few notes in response to these questions or have a conversation with a friend about them.

- *How do I naturally let go of tension?*
- *When I'm feeling centered, I feel _____ in my body.*
- *When I'm feeling well, how do I love to exalt and be with my body?*
- *If I utterly accepted my body [just imagine what that would be like!], then I would _____ and that would help me _____.*

> Life organizing doesn't require you to be quiet, to be solemn, or to have a chunk of time. It is to be used in the midst of all the insanity — that's the whole point!

Menu of Body Arts

Here's a sampling of ideas to prime your creative juices so you can create your own menu of simple body invitations. A tad of creative thinking will help you tune in to your body with greater richness and variety.

What's at Hand: Touch something and notice its texture. This can be your shirt, your skin, the couch you are lying on, the rug under your toes, the person sleeping next to you, the paper you are reading these words on.

Eavesdrop: Focus on a sound in your environment: bird song, wind in the trees, traffic, a child calling for her mother, the fridge whirring, music playing nearby, your partner talking in the next room.

Eyes On: Look at something closely: the texture of one finger, the color of your toenail polish, the way the light refracts through your water glass, the dancing dog in the print over the fireplace, the ad for debt relief over your head on the subway.

Prayer Hands: On an inhale, open your arms to your sides and then bring them overhead until your palms touch; on an exhale, bring your hands down in front of your heart.

Tension Extractor: Inhale and scrunch up your face, draw your shoulders to your ears, hunch over into a ball. Hold your breath for as long as you can, and with a loud exhale through your mouth, let go, flinging your arms open and imagining yourself as butter melting on hot, fresh popcorn.

Liberate Your Neck: Allow your head to hang forward like a ripening sunflower; breathe and very gently allow your shoulders to drop away from your neck. Move your neck gently from side to side, in small, kind movements.

Ear Love: Massage the outsides of your ears, from top to bottom. If you like, stick your fingers in your ears and listen to the sound of your breath for a moment.

Crown Pull: Place your thumbs on your temples and your fingers at your hairline, near your part. Pull your fingers firmly toward your thumbs, and imagine yourself opening your head and allowing anything that needs to be released flying out and away.

Repeat over your entire head by moving your thumbs and fingers back an inch or so until you have "pulled open" your head from the front to the back of your neck — let your pressure be firm (adapted from Donna Eden's *Energy Medicine*).

Buzz: Put your fingers in your ears, as if a friend were about to tell you how a movie you haven't seen yet ends. Inhale, and on your exhale, make a buzzing sound, as if you were a peaceful bee going about her business, content in the knowledge that she is in the right place, doing the right thing.

Oh Head: Place one hand on your forehead and the other on the back of your head. Inhale, and as you exhale, let out a loud, long "ah" or "oh" sound.

Here is an example of one way you can combine body moves to enliven your energy:

Inhale, and on your exhale, sigh (as loud and as long as your surroundings allow). Do Liberate Your Neck. On an inhale, slowly straighten your neck and lift your arms overhead, interlacing your fingers, with your palms pointing toward the ceiling. Exhale. On your next inhale, stretch your hands up while your shoulders descend as if someone were gently pulling your shoulder blades down.

Finish with Ear Love.

Time needed: one minute, or as long as you like.

> The body is the quickest way — to listen, to change, to energize.
>
> *Change your posture, your breathing, the way your eyes are focused; release the tension in your body; go outside for five minutes; touch something alive; eat something raw; drink a glass of water.*

Step 2: Feel

Science has confirmed the wisdom of what Luke asked in the New Testament, "What reason ye in your hearts?" Author Joseph Chilton Pearce stated in an interview, "Discoveries in the field of neurocardiology are, believe me, far more awesome than the discovery of nonlocality in quantum mechanics. It is the biggest issue of the whole century, but it's so far out and so beyond the ordinary, conceptual grasp, that a lot of the people doing the actual research are yet to be fully aware of the implications." The heart has its own independent nervous system with around forty thousand neurons (60 to 65 percent of all the cells in the heart are neural cells) — a "heart brain."

Neurocardiologists and other researchers are discovering that the heart is the psychophysiological means to create the life you want. The heart provides the most effective way to affect your physical health, your emotional well-being, your cognitive abilities, and, for our purposes, your ability to listen to greater wisdom and to direct your life by that wisdom. And there is strong evidence that by connecting with your heart (by consciously bringing up a pleasant feeling like love or appreciation), you affect others around you. Your heart produces $2\frac{1}{2}$ watts of electrical energy each time it beats, creating an electromagnetic field identical to the electromagnetic field around the earth. This field takes on a torus, or an egglike donut shape, that extends beyond your body from three to twenty-five feet. Chilton Pearce and others speculate that we may be able to link our hearts with those of others, perhaps using the holographic nature of the torus to promote well-being in others. At the very least, this practice of tuning in to your heart dramatically reduces stress, improves your creativity, and helps you feel more at peace and compassionate.

Neurocardiology proves what yoga sage Patanjali prescribed in the second century C.E.: put your attention on wholesome states. Soak in love, compassion, and creativity, and in time the ways of seeing and feeling that produce suffering will fall away and the wholesome states will remain. When you focus on love and appreciation, your "heart brain" affects your cranial brain; it actually changes your brain structurally, creating new neural pathways that make it easier to feel positive and to return to this positive state more quickly when you are stressed, exhausted, or in pain. Your cortisol levels fall, and your immune system may get a boost — in other words, you physically become what you are feeling!

The heart is the key to making life organizing work. First connect (engage the body), then focus on your heart (it helps me to place my hand there), and remember a moment in which you felt how you want to feel now, in the present moment. If you want to feel calm, perhaps you can remember kayaking with your best friend. If you want to feel creative, perhaps recall a moment in which you were brainstorming with co-workers and were bursting with fresh ideas. If you want to communicate clearly, your memory might be of an intimate conversation in which you listened and spoke with love. If coming up with a memory or a feeling feels difficult or you are drawing a blank, focus on a time when you felt appreciated or appreciative. Let yourself be shifted toward how you want to feel right now. This isn't about forcing; it's about inviting.

> Remember, it can be as simple as taking a conscious breath, checking in with your heart, and asking, "What do I want?"

This simple invitation opens a communication channel to wisdom beyond your thinking mind and your current perceptions of your situation. "The heart listens and receives and then it hands off to the mind to help things happen," is how Sufi master teacher and the author of *Unveiling the Heart of Your Business* Mark Silver described it to me. "The mind is not a sensing organ; it can't take in the unknown." By tapping into how you want to feel, you stop trying to think your way to a solution or new perspective and instead use your heart to intuit and feel your way. As you do, you biologically "entrain" yourself to this new place.

Menu of Heart Arts

The following ideas may aid you in connecting with your heart and making the emotional shift. The most important thing to remember — as with just about everything in life organizing — is that you already know how to do this. It isn't something new or difficult; you are simply bringing more attention to influencing how you feel for the purpose of guiding your life.

Don't Name It: The heart brain doesn't use language, so don't waste time trying to name how you want to feel; that engages the cranial brain. Remember: heart first, head second.

Breathe into It: Many practices, such as yoga, instruct us to breathe into and out of the heart area. Imagine your heart opening and closing, or picture it having a little pair of lungs.

Inner Heart Spot: Touch the center of your breastbone, and you'll find a slight hollow; it might even feel tender to the touch. In the yogic tradition, it is taught that your inner heart lies behind this spot. Gently rub or tap this area, then focus your breath there.

Bloom: Visualize or feel a flower (it can be a lotus, a rose, a peony — you choose) inside your chest, right at your heart. As you inhale, imagine the flower gently beginning to open, spreading its petals. With each exhale, focus on the shape of the flower, on the sensation of dwelling inside the blossom, or even on the scene or color. Enjoy a few breaths watching your heart bloom.

Step 3: Inquire

Asking questions is how we think — it's part of the narrative process of making meaning that our brains use to construct some semblance of reality. You ask yourself questions all the time: What do I want to wear today? What am I hungry for? What does this person want from me? Do I have to do that? These questions are mostly invisible to you, and yet they direct your attention. The questions you ask yourself influence your thoughts; your thoughts influence your mood; and your mood influences what you believe or feel is possible — that is, the actions you take. Marilee Adams, in *Change Your Questions, Change Your Life*, summed it up well: "The ability to intentionally shift our internal questions puts us in charge of our own thoughts."

> Cultivate an attitude of "I don't know" when life organizing. This attitude opens the gates, allowing fresh insight to come.

Asking heart-expanding questions is, of course, part of most spiritual traditions. Some schools of Buddhism have koans; Catholicism has catechism; in Hinduism we have Ramakrishna's ultimate meditative question, "Who am I?" We can look at all the wisdom traditions as varied responses to the question "How can I live as an honest and honorable person? How can I live to my full potential? How can I live with others?"

Asking questions of real worth can penetrate your self-limiting stories about who you are and what is possible like nothing else can — especially when coupled with an awakened body and a soft heart. You're using three of the most powerful tools human beings have — while working with your brain and body to create greater health on all levels. Think about it: the scientific puzzle of whether light is a particle or a wave was resolved when physicists understood that light appears as a wave if they ask a "wavelike question" and it appears as a particle if they ask a "particlelike question." The question itself affects the observer, who affects the answer.

So it makes sense that the next life-organizing step is asking a question of your enlivened body and your softened heart. But you're not asking just any question. You'll want to ask what I call a mindful question, a question that invites you not to find the answer, but rather to see or sense fresh possibilities. You are not trying to find *the correct solution*. That works well in some areas, such as medicine, math, engineering, or biology, for example, but in most areas of life, there is rarely one correct solution, and thinking there is can cause you a tremendous amount of suffering and can dam your creative juices. Asking mindful questions can help shift your perspective on whatever you are inquiring about, enabling you to see (or intuit or sense or hear or feel) what you couldn't before. This is possible because of how you have worded

> The questions you ask shape the story you live.
>
> *What story do you want to live?*

the questions, because you have connected to your heart, and because you are willing to inhabit and breathe the question instead of demanding an answer. (See Allow, p. 28.)

Mindful Questions for Every Day

Use these questions for in-the-moment life organizing and whenever you need to make a choice throughout your day. Some of these questions are terrific to ask when you're feeling off, out of it, overwhelmed, clutching, clenching, judgmental, fearful, exhausted, shut down, small, like you're living in a box, focused on what other people need or want from you, or in any way cut off from the present moment.

- *What is this moment calling from me?*

This is one of my all-time favorite come-into-the-moment questions, created by master coach Molly Gordon.

- *What do I need to know right now?*

Focus on doing things one step at a time instead of on knowing the big picture. What if you really don't need to know more than the next step?

- *What do I want?*

This is one of the most powerful questions — and one of the scariest. Remind yourself that you don't have to act on what you want, that wanting doesn't mean getting, and that the ultimate creativity is being in touch with your undiluted desires.

- *What don't I want?*

Sometimes using the process of elimination can be a less intimidating way to inch forward than naming what you do want.

- *How can I be gentle with myself in this situation?*

We can all benefit from asking this many times a day.

- *What does my body need right now?*

Instead of saying, "I'm thirsty, but first I'll answer this email/wipe this bottom/empty the dishwasher," honor the gift of flesh you've been given, and pour yourself a tall glass of water right now.

- *Spirit, what do I need right now?*

This is a great question for increasing your relationship to what can't be known or named. Of course, substitute whatever word for Spirit works for you.

- *What am I not allowing myself to know?*

This question works well when you are feeling rested, safe, or brave enough to know. Try asking it while in the bath, on a long walk, during a yoga or exercise class, or when drifting off to sleep.

- *Where does my energy want to go next?*

Ask this question, then simply follow where your energy leads you.

- *How do I choose to spend my energy and time?*

This is the perfect question to ask when faced with a decision or an invitation. The answer might be no, I don't want to do that, and you might *still* go ahead and do it, but your ability to resent and blame others will disappear because you chose.

- *What's most important in this moment?*

This is effective to ask in high-stress situations, including business and family management.

- *What choice will keep me sane?*
- *What would I be proud of?*
- *What can I be satisfied with?*
- *How can I nurture myself today?*

Ask yourself this question first thing in the morning.

- *What would I most like to create next?*
- *Is this what I really want right now?*

Ask these questions when you are about to choose something that might not be in your best interest. See Shadow Comforts and Time Monsters (p. 41) for more pointers.

- *Is there something else I would rather be doing?*
- *What am I getting out of being so busy/frantic/overwhelmed?*

Ask these when you are in the midst of insanity. Gently.

- *How can I give myself permission to enjoy this moment?*

This is also an in-the-moment question and is usually one of pleasure, fun, or intimate connection (try asking yourself this question during sex).

Step 4: Allow

Allowing is a fluid, ever-changing *experience* because it involves communion with the mysterious. Your mind wants you to listen only to it, or at the very least, to listen to it before anything else. But your experience has taught you there are far vaster fields of information that you can open your awareness to and that, in fact, one of the quickest routes to a life you don't love is listening to and relying solely on your mind, or on what Carl Jung called the small self.

Allowing becomes infinitely easier and more rewarding because you are connected to your body, heart, and mind (connect, feel, inquire). Each element works together. On a practical note that means if it feels hard to allow guidance or to relax, connect with your body and your heart.

> Make a list of all the times that inner guidance or knowing has been helpful, even lifesaving, to you. Put this list in the front of your Life Planner.

My favorite stories are those of women listening to and following their inner promptings, finding the true shape of their lives: Anne Morrow Lindbergh going on a seaside retreat, Isak Dinesen falling in love with Africa and, finally, herself; Shirley Valentine luxuriating on a Grecian beach; May Sarton arranging flowers each morning; Tillie Olson writing between cooking and ironing; Annie Dillard finding refuge in her one-room cabin on an island in the Northwest. These women claimed themselves, and what they had to offer the world, partly by opening to the infinite, whether the infinite was God, writing, poetry, Greek olives, the Ngong Hills, or hot sand and turquoise waves. I keep these stories and others on a shelf in my studio so I can be reminded, just by glancing at the books, that I am not alone in my quest to allow life to move through me, to find expression through my gifts, to live fully.

> We so often expect "spiritual" or nontangible experiences to be otherworldly, profound, or ecstatic. This sort of thinking snarls the life-organizing process. Let this process be as mundane as checking email or as profound as hearing an angel's voice — information comes to us *constantly* but we block it because it isn't explicit or spectacular enough, because we do not like what we hear, or because we haven't learned our own language of guidance, which we learn only through experience!

Allowing means being willing to lean into your question with wonder and trusting that it will take you where you most need to go in this instance. Allowing means you are willing to open a conduit to that which you cannot measure or see — it might be all you have experienced in your life, the vital information filed away in various storage spots around your mind and body because your conscious mind can't possibly keep it all front and center (that would be psychosis). You may open to bodily wisdom, an immense source of knowing that starts with the fact that muscles have a memory and ends in the wilds of concepts like cellular and ancestral memory. You may open to Big Mind (which is without size or limits, has no beginning and no end, no birth and no death), or the collective unconscious, or Source, or God, or Allah. In the end, what you open to doesn't matter; it's your *experience* of listening to and seeing where that leads you — of noticing and tracking your experiences, of deciding what works and what to trust — that counts. Allowing is not about belief: it's about experience and noticing that experience. That is how you create a life you love right *now*. It never fails to thrill me that when I am willing to stop and let go of my need to know, guidance in some form always comes to me.

Step 5: Apply

The process of applying is straightforward and concrete — you apply what you receive, as soon as possible. Overthinking, especially when you first start using this process, can cause you to doubt or to push away what you have received. This practice is not about taking big steps — it's about taking *some* action, no matter how small, in line with what has occurred to you. Taking small actions of trust builds your "trust muscles," which helps you to become even more adept at allowing. Tracking what insights come to you and what happens when you follow those insights brings discernment and decreases magical thinking — especially when you keep notes in your Life Planner or the Life Organizer app. (See Fruits of the Heart, p. 232.) In a nutshell, this is what St. Loyola was advocating in sixteenth-century Spain in his *Spiritual Exercises*. Pay attention to where your inner desires are taking you; notice how you feel and what manifests in your life as you move closer to or away from these desires.

Applying means taking an *actual physical action* or clearly declaring when you will take action. In *Getting Things Done*, David Allen points out that one of the ways we overwhelm ourselves is by writing down projects or outcomes on our calendars instead of the "very next physical actions required to move the situation forward." A project is "write a novel," "research assisted living for Mom," or "buy a new couch." These need to be broken down into actual doable steps like "write for ten minutes about what my novel might be about" or "call Patti and ask her where her mother lives" or "make a list of stores to visit on Saturday" or "choose a color scheme." This sort of thinking, when coupled with trusting the guidance that comes to you, creates an immense amount of focus and inner-directed forward momentum.

For more examples of what this might look like, see Ideas for Your Planner (p. 68) and the stories scattered throughout the Life Planner.

Life-Planning Concepts

The five steps of connect, feel, inquire, allow, and apply enable you to create your optimum life day by day, moment by moment. The life-planning concepts — intention, life insights, desire, shadow comforts and time monsters, minimum requirements for self-care, and story — help you see and sustain the larger picture. Think of the five steps as your stitches and the six concepts as your pattern. The pattern gives you a guideline, and the stitches intimately bring to life — and therefore change — what the pattern has prescribed. Let's explore these "pattern" concepts now.

Intention

Your intention describes what you want. It's the focus for your energy *and* the needle in your compass; you direct your energy toward when you lose your way, feel overwhelmed, or need to choose which direction to move in. It helps you choose in service to your heart instead of as dictated by your mind. One definition of the word *intend* is "to stretch your thoughts toward something"; a definition of *intention* is "an aim that guides your choices." An intention keeps you gently focused on what you want to experience and embody during a particular chunk of time (an hour, a day, a month) or event (a yoga class, a meeting, a party, your house renovation), *and* it creates a space for your energy to gather.

My friend Marcie Telander, a therapist and storyteller, talks about the rawhide "possible bag" created for Plains Indian boys and girls for their rite of passage. The bag will be filled, over the course of his or her life, with life skills, discoveries, and medicine tools. It's a possibility space, flexible and yet clearly delineated. You can think of intention as your "possible bag" — as thoughts and feelings that create a place for what is possible to gather, a sacred space for your life skills, discoveries, and medicine tools to congregate and guide you. If you feel scattered, or that your focus is on what others need (or what you think they need), or that you give away so much of yourself that there is little left over for you, using intention is a gentle way to bring your energy back to yourself, and then to decide where to direct it.

An intention can be a short phrase or a mindful question. My weekly intentions have included "praising myself," "listening for direction for my book project," and "staying playfully focused," and they can be questions like "What is the most loving use of my time this week?" "How can I be kind to myself in each moment?" and "What might be a fair response?" Asking intention questions is a powerful way of tuning in to greater wisdom throughout the day; so is simply having a phrase or word that you keep bringing to your attention.

To add additional power to your intentions, you can write them on your Life Planner pages or use the app you can download at jenniferlouden/lifeorganizer. When you do, take a moment to feel (with hand on heart, breathing and recalling a loving or appreciative moment), and then imagine your intention radiating out from your enlivened heart and into the world via the energy of your heart torus. Feel your intention being blessed and amplified by your heart energy. If you wish, you might imagine your heart torus intersecting with the heart torus of someone you love or even with the universal torus, thus giving you all the information and energy you could ever need to realize your intention.

Life Insights

You've got the gray hairs to show for them, so why not find a way to benefit from your lifelong insights? Remembering and applying them can save you from wasting time (years!), money, energy, and love. Yet most of us were never taught to track, record, and refer to what we learn in life, or to hone these insights as they change and grow with us. This is a waste!

Life insights are gifted to you through therapy, coaching, reading, studying, meditation, prayer, spiritual practices, and listening to something larger than yourself. They tend to become clear on retreats, during long walks or runs, when we are rowing or folding laundry, during conversations with perceptive friends and sometimes enigmatic strangers, and when we are writing or creating art. Sometimes we spot them in our journal, on our canvases, and in our complaints. We gather them through living, and often through pain, especially the third or tenth or thirtieth time around.

Below you will learn about minimum requirements for self-care. The difference between these and life insights is that life insights are the distillation of a life lesson. Minimum requirements grow out of these insights. For example, suppose "yoga heals me" is my insight; it then spawns the minimum requirement to do some yoga every day. Minimum requirements are the activities, practices, and things that help you remember your insights and live your life by their wisdom, but they are not the same thing. To remember your insights every day would be overkill, and who has time for that anyway?

Go on a search for your life insights, and create a list. Your goal is not to list everything you have learned — that might be a tad overwhelming. Instead, you want to gather five to ten insights *that feel vital to you right now*. You may be able to come up with a list in a few minutes of free writing, or by walking and thinking, or by having a conversation with a perceptive friend. Or you might need to dig around more — most of us do, at least to find the painful life insights we really don't want to remember but that would be helpful in the days and months ahead. In that case, get out your magnifying glass and proceed with an attitude of absolute self-compassion and love. No self-cruelty permitted!

Searching for Insights

- Revisit old journals and look for recurrent themes — you might want to use Post-its to capture insights, choosing a color for each particular theme, like pink for body, blue for nature, and so on.

- Look over photographs of significant moments in your life.

- Check in with your current or former therapist(s), spiritual director, minister, or coach and ask them, "What have you heard me say I don't ever want to forget? What life lessons have you watched me learn?"

- Think of someone who really bugs you, and then ask yourself what he or she is doing that you would never do. Write it down. Now look at what you wrote: Is there any life insight there that you may have forgotten? For example, I have a friend who is always late and disorganized. I write down how much that's bugging me, and I realize I've forgotten one of my own life insights: to leave a margin of time and energy around what I'm doing, especially during deadlines.

- Study your bookshelves: what books are you drawn to? Why did you buy these particular volumes? Hold a book without opening it, and let the most important thing you have learned from it come into your awareness. Repeat this exercise with a few different treasured volumes.

- When you look back at what you consider your most painful life moments, what life lesson would you say you have learned? Or what life lesson did you ignore? You could explore one painful episode or period in your past by free-writing for fifteen minutes. Then use a highlighter to illuminate any key insights or important words.

- What issue or challenge has arisen in your life recently that made you say to yourself, "I thought I learned that a long time ago"?

- What do you consider the most important lesson you learned from your parents or community or religious tradition?

Narrow It Down

If you have compiled a massive tome of everything you've learned, you'll want to copy only three to five of the insights *you currently want to pay attention to* into your Life Planner. Put them where you can see them from time to time — like on the front cover or near the beginning or on a large Post-it note you can use like a bookmark.

Desire

On most of the Life Planner pages, you'll encounter questions like "What do I desire this week?" "What calls to me, even if it doesn't make logical sense or I'm certain I don't have the time or energy for it?" "If I were suddenly infused with twenty times more courage, what would I want this week? What depth of desire might reveal itself to me?" Almost every "week" a question or two asks you to consider what you desire, how you want to explore and shape the life force coursing through you. Why such a focus on desire? Because it's pure life force speaking to you, and we have neglected and misunderstood it for far too long. The Indo-European root of the word *cherish* is *ka*. According to Joseph Shipley, in *The Origins of English*

> Desire helps you gently bypass the inner struggle that can block ease and flow.

Words, ka meant "desire." In Latin, *ka* morphed into *caritas,* or *love.* Shipley suggests that in the First Epistle of Paul, *caritas,* was transliterated instead of translated, so the passage should read: "And now abideth faith, hope, desire, these three; but the greatest of these is desire" (instead of "And now abideth faith, hope, charity, these three; but the greatest of these is charity"). (See Fruits of the Heart, p. 232, for more.) St. Augustine said, "Thy desire is thy prayer and if thy desire is without ceasing, thy prayer will be without ceasing. . . . The continuance of your longing is the continuance of your prayer," and the contemporary Indian teacher Sri Nisargadatta said, "The problem is not desire. It's that your desires are too small." Desire is the flow of life we yearn to swim in, the urge to be one with Spirit, *and the way to stay in touch with this flow is through knowing what we want without insisting that we get it.* It is staying with the feeling of desire, following it with curiosity, that leads us ever closer to what we most want. All desire, at its heart, is about a longing to be loved and to be one with All That Is. Even the most mundane desires or, worse, ones that have calcified into unhealthy obsessions have at their root this desire to be known and loved.

> When I was speaking in Seattle about life organizing, a charming man asked me, "I feel like I'm settling for too little. What if I really want to make ten million dollars? I don't act on what I want because I'm afraid I'm settling." I said, "Stop thinking about the big picture. What do you want right now? Trust that, keep listening to that."

Yet desire is often misunderstood — confused with greed, lust, narcissism — and especially pertinent to our discussion, with an attachment to a particular outcome. In *Open to Desire*, Mark Epstein advises us to think of desire as "teacher." When we confuse desiring with having or attaining something, we move away from ourselves, away from listening-flowing-feeling-creating and into the pushing, striving, teeth-gritting, forcing way of being. Most of us are fabulous at making things *happen*, but when we disconnect from the energy of desire, the sensuous ever-changing rumba of life can become a syncopated rigid march that we have to perform — and, often, perfectly. Desire becomes a place to get to rather than a vital energy to feel, experience, and ride.

Psychoanalyst and writer Adam Phillips notes in *Darwin's Worms* that there seem to be two kinds of people in the world, "those that can enjoy desiring and those who need satisfaction." When we insist that we will feel desire only if that desire can be satisfied exactly as we wish it to be, we grow smaller. "It is possible to be in a state in which desire is valued, not as a prelude to possession, control, or merger but as a mode to appreciation itself," states Epstein. To desire a gorgeous garden, a soul mate, deep inner peace, the ability to play Chopin, that your loved ones live a long, happy life is to feel life rising in you like sap, exhilarating, rushing, impossibly sweet, and unstoppable. The calcifying of the desire into a must-have, an accomplishment — whether it be a custom-built house or a safari or a sculpture you made that brings others to tears — is very different and is the reason desire has gotten a bad rap. That kind of desire becomes fuel for greed and grasping. But when desire and the light of awareness meet, we can experience desire as energy, fuel, and Spirit speaking to us, and then it can play a very different role.

I must digress to add that as women, many of us carry an extra layer of fear in regard to desire — brought on by the cultural edict that good women don't want. When I lead retreats and work with the subject of desire, I am constantly amazed by the stories of women who have been forced, usually when they were children, to cut themselves off from desire, to regard it as too dangerous, as something that only brings trouble and suffering. To want means to be disappointed or, even worse, to be hurt, shamed, degraded. History is replete with women who were forced to downplay or forgo their desires — many of us have seen our mothers, aunts, or grandmothers live this way — and there are far too many heartbreaking stories of women being punished for wanting. Our world seems to hold out choice with one hand and rescind it with the other, so we may decide it is safer to channel our energy into what we think we should do (make money, raise super-achieving kids, work out and starve ourselves till we're a size 0). I tell you this to invite you to be aware of any conflicting feelings you may have about desire. It is imperative that you become aware of any little voices whispering in your ear that you can't trust desire, that it's better to play it safe, that it's best not to want, not to take a risk and be disappointed.

Mindful Desire Questions

- *How do I know what I want?*

To know what you want is first to know how to know, to become an expert on your own guidance system. How do you know what you want? By a whisper in your ear? A warmth in your solar plexus? A twinge deep in your gut? Goose bumps? Dreams? An idea that won't go away?

Try this: make a list of things you have wanted in the past — anything that comes to mind. List twenty things. Then, on the right-hand side of the paper, record how you knew you wanted that thing, person, or experience. See if you can, even vaguely, recall how you knew.

Or go through one day noticing how you know what you want — to eat, to drink, to wear, to touch, to kiss, to read, to watch, to listen to, to be around, to see, to talk to. What signals let you know this? How often are they shoulds or have-tos versus true desires? How often do you override what you want in favor of something "safer" or "more right"? How often do you tell yourself, "I can't because so-and-so needs me"? Be incredibly curious and compassionate with yourself. Many of us have never asked ourselves how we know what we want. It's vital information.

> Life organizing is the perfect refuge when you don't know what to do next or when your day is falling apart or when you don't want to do anything on your to-do list.

- *What would I experience, create, and feel if I had no excuses?*

Try taking three sweet mindful breaths and asking Spirit to show you. Then write, sketch, collage, dance, or speak every response that comes to you for a certain period of time — ten minutes or thirty minutes, or even an hour if you are working with art media. If your critical or bossy self butts in, tell her she can have her say later; right now you are listening to a higher Source.

- *What would I love to make the next hour (or half hour or five minutes) be about?*

This question comes from Michael Neill, coach and author of *You Can Have What You Want*. Ask it often.

Shadow Comforts and Time Monsters

A shadow comfort is anything that masquerades as a cherishing self-care technique but in fact drains your energy. Shadow comforts fuel the story that you can't be trusted to be good to yourself and that using hard-ass discipline is the best way to run your life. Shadow comforts can take any form. It's not what you do; it's *why* you do it that makes the difference. You can eat a piece of chocolate as a holy wafer of sweetness — a real comfort — or you can cram an entire chocolate bar into your mouth without even tasting it in a frantic attempt to soothe yourself — a shadow comfort. You can chat on message boards for half an hour and be energized by community and ready to go back to work, or you can chat on message boards because you're avoiding talking to your partner about how angry he or she made you last night.

Maybe you're asking, "What's the difference between a habit and a shadow comfort?" This is a complicated question. Some habits are physical addictions (like smoking) and may require outside intervention to change; I see habits as unintentional practices. I'm practicing something; thus I'm teaching myself something. When I check my email every few minutes, I'm teaching myself how to think shallowly and training myself to feel content with answering email instead of working on a chunk of a larger, more challenging project. When I choose to eat chocolate instead of feeling my feelings, I'm teaching myself avoidance and that emotions are scary. You could check email and be teaching yourself to stay on top of your workload — again, it's not what you do; it's why you do it, and what results you experience.

When I look at my habits as practices, as *something I am teaching myself*, instead of as fatal flaws that I can never change, I create enough space to identify what I am doing that doesn't feel nourishing. Then, if I choose to, I can move into the mood of being a creator, of shaping my life, by asking one of these questions:

- *Is this teaching me what I want to learn?*
- *Is this helping me live my truest life?*
- *Is this giving me energy?*

And the most powerful question of all:

- *What do I really want?*

Helga, a single mother and early Life Organizer user, wrote that for her shadow comforts are the "behaviors I choose to numb myself when I'm in too much pain or fear. The phenomenon as such is actually a built-in, healthy emotional response when it serves as temporary self-preservation during a serious onslaught (like losing a loved one). But they turn into shadow comforts when they become chronic or habitual or kick in at the slightest discomfort."

Closely related but slightly different from shadow comforts are time monsters — anything we pretend is a creative, generative use of our time but is actually a way to dodge doing what we really want to do. We all have things we don't want to do but that we need to do (like paying bills), or maybe we want to take a risk (like starting a new painting), and yet neither of these activities feels easy or comfortable. So instead we make an elaborate dinner every night for our family, spend a week choosing the perfect font for the flyer for the annual neighborhood picnic, or become news junkies who have to read three newspapers and check five news sites every morning and don't understand why we never seem to have enough time.

I've coached many women whose lives consisted almost entirely of time monsters because they were too afraid to do what they really wanted to do — for fear of failure, for fear of what their mother/ husband/children might think, for fear that when their long-held dream was realized it would become tarnished by daily living. The stories that these women created to allow them to live this way were full of conviction, and they held on to them with great determination. Spending a month planning and cooking and decorating for the holidays, spending a week decorating your child's classroom, insisting that every trip be meticulously scrapbooked, running unnecessary errands: we tell ourselves that we must do these things and that in fact we are the only ones who *can* do them. We spend our lives doing things that don't matter, and meanwhile our desires are sobbing, locked away in the basement.

There are subtle differences between time monsters and overcommitting that are critical to discern. You can overcommit to things you don't really want to do to avoid the life you're afraid to live (time monsters); you can overcommit to something because you can't say no out of fear of disappointing someone or being judged as selfish; and you can overcommit because you are such a glorious polymath, bursting with so many interests and passions, that you forget you live in a human body and thus have limits on your energy and time. Of course, all these boondoggles can overlap and tangle you into a heap of "Who cares? Let's watch TV and forget all about this creating-a-life crap." Here is where shadow comforts excel — lulling you into the belief that numbness is the safest choice. Clever, aren't they?

Life organizing necessitates that you learn to discern how you spend your precious energy — but you must do this with infinite mercy. Weep with tenderness for the parts of you that are dedicated to keeping you busy and numb. Compassionately embrace the truth that you don't do this work only once. You get to do it again and again, and then again. The good news is that time monsters and shadow comforts do loosen their hold and can disappear entirely; mostly, they simply appear less frequently and become subtler — which is plenty of shift, let me tell you. The Life Planner excels at helping you see this spiral of growth clearly and encourages you to muster bountiful wide-hearted mercy for yourself along the way.

Here are some fundamental discerning questions to consider. You will refer back to them as you use the Life Planner, so respond to them when you are ready (which will be more than once, since your responses will change as you change).

Mindful Shadow Comfort and Time Monster Questions

- *What are my current favorite shadow comforts and the four or five situations or feelings that trigger my need for them?*

Do you turn to these comforts when someone yells at you, when your child is surly or out of control, when the scale says you have gained instead of lost, when the pain in your back is bugging you, after a hard day at work, when you are around people who drain your energy or criticize you? Do you find yourself saying, "I deserve this ice cream and TV" in those situations?

- *What are my favorite time monsters?*

Remember that a time monster can be anything that feels urgent or that leads you to wonder why you are spending so much time doing it or to saying, "Just one more minute, and then I'll stop."

- *When do I let my time monsters take over my life?*

Time monsters often crop up during times of transition (when you're home from work, after the dishes are done at night, on Friday and Sunday nights), when you don't have something clear or urgent to do, when you are anxious and putting something off — especially if what you are avoiding is creative and risky.

Minimum Requirements for Self-Care

Between surviving and leading a fully humming creative life lies the middle ground of determining your minimum requirements for self-care, a duded-up way of saying what you absolutely must have to stay in touch with your center. Basic needs, or minimum requirements, are different for each woman, although getting enough sleep, moving our bodies, eating fresh food, being touched, and connecting to something larger than ourselves show up pretty consistently on women's lists — but again, not on everybody's. It can be easy to discount the importance of these basics, because getting enough alone time or napping when you are tired just doesn't sound as sexy as realizing some fabulous dream. Yet without these basics, the dreams don't come true, or you can't sustain them when they do, or, most tragically, it turns out that you are following not your dreams but rather a script about what you *should* do. But when you reach a certain stage of commitment to yourself, you find that you are willing to give the amount of attention and energy needed to these basics, because without them, it isn't your life. You discover that you have less leeway to stray from what is essential.

Give yourself time to find your minimum requirements. Allow yourself to notice and adjust them. You may start out with ten things and find that all you really need is to get seven hours of sleep, to remember to breathe and listen, and to touch living things.

Of course, minimum requirements change over time and with your situation. When my dad died, my minimums shrank to taking my vitamins and herbs, drinking water, and taking care of my daughter. I knew I would reevaluate what I needed after I grieved. The paradox here is your personalized list may be your treasure map home to your center, and sometimes you don't want or can't use it. But you can always find where you buried it. As Laraine said to me a few months after attending a Kripalu retreat with me,

> Making conscious what makes me feel good helps me recover more quickly from periods when I am denied these basics and helps me better tolerate not having them because I know when they will resume. The list is a good reminder to eat breakfast on the screened porch looking at the birds rather than in the dark kitchen listening to news on the radio or to reach out to friends for help and in the process find out they need help from me. The daily minimum requirements are a reminder of my strengths and individuality, my right to enjoy life, and the awareness that I am a better person by doing what I want.

By writing down your minimum requirements and then paying attention to your list — perhaps posting it where you can see it or when prompted by the Life Organizer app buddy — you become aware of what you are already doing to maintain your connection to self. You will also see what trips you up, and you can decide if you want to do anything about it. If you have a fear of self-care — that it will make you a pampered, selfish bitch, for instance — this sort of noticing moves you toward resiliency and taking more responsibility for your life. If you focus only on the big vision or on all you want to do, you can forget the basics; this focus on the ideal can keep you from getting where you want to go or from having enough energy to enjoy it once you get there. Are you resisting declaring minimum requirements out of fear that by not thinking big you limit your life's purpose? Then you may want to notice how keeping the channel to your wisdom open by tending to your basics beautifully influences your well-being — for the good of all.

Some Sample Minimum Daily Requirements: Mine and Dee's

Jennifer

Daily
Meditation, usually first thing in the morning
Physical movement, especially outdoors
Creating: writing, arranging flowers, dancing
Taking herbs and vitamins
Drinking lots of water; carrying water on errands
Getting eight hours of sleep
Hugging and touching other living things like my dogs
Reading for fun
Choosing what I want

Weekly
Watching for signs of having eaten too much sugar or being under
    too much stress
Seeing or talking to my mom and my daughter

Time alone
Using the Life Planner or other reflection
Learning something new

Monthly
Time to do nothing
Making "art messes"

Yearly
Spending time in nature with Bob unplugged
Learning something in-depth
Travel somewhere new

Dee

Daily
Enjoying a spiritual moment: drawing, praying, watching the bird
    feeders, gardening, choosing an angel card
Moving my body: dancing, doing aerobics, weight lifting, horseback
    riding, biking
Eating one meal that is all raw
Writing in my gratitude journal
Getting six hours of sleep
Spending time with my partner: nothing special, just being together

Weekly
Hiking in nature
Having one good connection with a friend or my sisters

Making time to "catch up" with my business expenses and home
   budget
Loving sex

Monthly
Spending a few hours in silence
Having a new experience: seeing a play, visiting a part of the city I've
   never been in, trying out a new recipe, taking a class

Yearly
Spending a week living close to the land: no technology allowed
Going on a retreat, led by a great teacher, with other women

Mindful Minimum Self-Care Questions

   Finding your style of balance starts by identifying what it means
and looks like for you and then weaving that knowledge into your
life by using the Life Planner.
• *Without _____, I lose myself.*
Make a list of your basic self-care requirements. Ask those you are
intimate with what they observe about you. The most common
are enough sleep; solitude; time with people I love; nature, especially
water; connection with a higher Source; creative musing for no
particular purpose; unscheduled time away from technology;
enough protein; and water. Give yourself a little time to be really
thorough.
• *When I feel most connected to my center, I am _____.*

- When I feel most connected to something larger than myself and my agenda, I am _____.
- My body helps me be connected when it has _____.
- I could live without _____ but not for long.

Mindful Balance Questions

- What is my vision of balance? Is there another word besides balance that fits me better?
- Would I know balance, or its equivalent, if it hit me over the head?
- Is my vision humanly possible? Or would I need six arms and to exist in multiple dimensions? If it is, when was the last time I experienced it? Did I truly enjoy it?
- What helps me live inside this vision, embody it, believe it?
- What personal alarms go off when I'm getting out of balance?

Make a list of your melt-down signals. Mine include itchy skin (a sign that I've eaten too much sugar), not meditating, not reading poetry, being dramatic about how much I have to do, and conducting a private conversation that goes something like "I should...," while my outer conversations include a lot of "I'm sorry I'm late, but..."

- What throws me out of balance during _____ time of the year?

Examples include winter holidays, tax season, sheep shearing (hey, it's a busy time), vacation (many people find so-called pleasure trips empty and disorienting), and anniversaries of a death or other loss. Look back to plan ahead.

- *How do I usually respond to stress? What choices do I sometimes make?*

Your answers could include losing your temper, eating everything in sight, drinking too much _____, adding an exercise class, praying, reaching out for help.

Story

The last of our life-organizing concepts is the most global. This concept could fill volumes, and the basics, presented here, have the power to revolutionize your life when you apply them.

You observe the world in your own way, a way formed by your biology, life experiences, education, culture, spiritual beliefs, and many other influences. That's a common enough idea — you observe the world through a lens fashioned from all these facets of you. Yet consider: *to observe is to interpret.* You literally cannot experience reality as it is, just like you can never see yourself without a mirror. You live in a world first filtered through your brain's system of sorting, editing, and ordering information and then shaped by your observations. It is a narrative system — information comes in, and your brain sorts it into a story, which is a good thing, since *400 billion* bits of information are received by your brain every *second.* Without this narrative-making brain, you would soon be insane. Creating narratives is how you make sense of things. Everything you experience is the product of this storytelling process; without really knowing it, you become the shape of your stories. You look at a person, and you see your story of him and *whatever meaning you assign him.* You start a business, and it fails, and you create a story out of those events. "We do not see how things are; we see them according to how *we are*," writes Australian coach Alan Sieler in *Coaching and the Human Soul*.

We can create tremendous pain in our lives, our communities, our corporations, and our world by confusing story with fact, interpretation with truth. When we believe that there is only one true religion or that one race is superior to others, for example, there is no limit to the evil we can perpetrate in the name of "truth." On a more intimate scale, how many of us are unhappy right this second because we believe our co-worker or boss or partner or child ought to be a certain way, in spite of the reality that he or she is not? How much time and energy do we spend nagging and hoping that people and circumstances be different than they are, more in alignment with our interpretation or story of what is *right*?

Given this powerful automatic dynamic it is critical to ask yourself these questions: What stories am I telling myself? What do I base these stories on? Do I base them in fact? What is fact and what is interpretation? How life giving are my stories? Is there a kinder story to be telling myself?

Here's an example of how powerfully the stories we tell can shape our lives. Having had my share of knee injuries and two surgeries, when my knee started "sticking" as I rode my bike, accompanied by a couple of sharp pains, I immediately assumed (or interpreted this to mean) that something was seriously wrong. On the ride home, I imagined a future in which hiking, yoga, and biking were gone and a knee replacement was looming.

Over the next few weeks, I stopped exercising. I ignored my knee, told myself I was getting old, and beat myself up for not being able to participate in extreme sports — never mind that I don't even *like* extreme sports. After a few weeks of telling myself this story, it finally occurred to me to go see Mark, an orthopedic surgeon, to have my knee checked out. He laid his hand on my knee, twisted it in each direction, and told me my knee was in solid shape and that I was most likely experiencing "wear and tear," and perhaps a small tear in my cartilage.

Oh.

Because of his *grounded* assessment of my knee, which was based on his years of training, and my trust in his ability, my mood and my use of my body changed — instantly. Suddenly, I was literally leaping around his office, flexing my knee, calculating how many yoga classes I could fit in that week. My interpretation of the sensation in my knee had changed — the twinge, the catch, the pain were no longer "serious," just due to wear and tear. *Yet the sensations were the same.* Before I walked into Mark's office, I was telling myself a story that I was broken and doomed. Ten minutes later, I was ready to climb Mt. Rainier. All that had changed was how I interpreted the pain.

Separating the Story from the Facts

To understand the power of stories, you need to cultivate a habit of noticing your interpretations and whether they are serving you. What if, instead of assuming that the sensations in my knee meant I was badly hurt, I had said to myself, "Hmm.... This is a new sensation. Let me take a moment to feel this. When I stand I feel a catch. My knee feels like I don't want anybody to touch it. I don't want to ride a bike or do deep knee bends." When I remain with the sensation in my knee, without having to decide what it means, my field of possibilities widens dramatically. When I decide that my interpretation of an experience or sensation is a fact and *I forget I'm making up an interpretation, forget that I am observing through the lens of me,* my ability to shape my life becomes cramped and limited, or it shuts down altogether. When I believed my own story that there was something wrong with my knee, my mind went instantly about its job of proving my story to be true. When I don't observe the story as simply that, a story, it becomes *the truth.* Often we observe without being aware of the context that shapes our observations, just as a fish isn't aware it lives in water (or at least I don't think the fish is aware). Water just "is," and many of our interpretations have that same quality of inevitability: this is just the way I am, this is just the way working in this company is, this is how I always feel when my mother comes into town. Oh really? Is that true? *This* is rarely anything other than an interpretation.

Here's another story: after being in my office writing since very early, I went into the kitchen to make breakfast — and found a mess my family had left. In the past, I would have known it was *wrong* and *bad* for them to have not done the dishes before going out to play soccer. I mean, they left the syrup out! But now I can ask, "Where is that written? Is that a law, like gravity, or even a moral injunction like love your neighbor?" This doesn't mean that I choose to clean up the kitchen — although if I'm waiting for my tea to brew, I might, at least a little — nor does it mean that I can't make a request like "I really feel icky when the kitchen is messy all morning. Can you clean up after yourselves?" That's all good, but it doesn't make my story — that a good family has a clean kitchen and if my family listened to me, they would hold to my standards 100 percent of the time — true. When I can see this as my story, then poof! My suffering and my need to yell at my family about how they take advantage of me evaporate. I have noticed my story and realized that the only thing holding it in place is my image of a family life that I don't even really believe in. When I'm aware and stop to feel, I realize that I would never trade in the peace and warmth of an imperfectly human connection for this unrealistic image.

Cheat Sheet for Observing Your Stories

Because your mind will *always* work to prove that its story is the truth, it can be almost impossible to think your way out of a story. Before you have fully begun to question your interpretations, your mind has amassed impressive justifications for believing your painful version of reality. One potent remedy is to write your thoughts down, since writing helps you detach from your story. Here are some questions to help get you started.

• *What is my interpretation of this?*
"This" can be anything: a sensation in your body, a person, an event, a work of art, a tone of voice, the weather, the president, you name it. Jot down a few words — adjectives come into play here, as do value judgments, like what's right or good and what's wrong or bad.

About the pain in my knee, I would write: deterioration, limitation, weakness, end of well-being.

About the breakfast mess I would jot down: laziness, disrespect, sloppiness, chaos, exhaustion, and burden.

- *What are the facts?*

The facts in my kitchen story include that a dirty skillet is on the range and dishes with bits of egg and syrup are on the counter, along with the syrup bottle. The facts about my knee include that when I make certain motions with my knee, I feel certain sensations. When you look for facts, you look for things that someone else with the same cultural background could see or agree with. The temperature is 68 degrees. My eyes are blue. There are dishes on the counter. My boss said, "You're fired." Delineating between facts and stories is one of the most powerful life practices you can develop. It is also pretty tricky because we wander back into stories (remember, that is how our brain works!) so easily. "My boss said, 'You're fired'" immediately morphs into "I'm incompetent" or "Nobody understands me."

Having someone to talk to who can help you look for the facts can be indispensable. (Remember the fish! A friend or therapist or coach can point out the water that we don't see.) Facts can be objectively measured and will be agreed on by all parties who share the same standards and tools of measurement. How would you prove to someone else that you are not smart enough? It may be a fact that you flunked algebra, but does that really prove that you aren't smart enough to run your business? To get a master's degree (presumably in something other than higher mathematics)? It may be a fact that you did not go to college, but how does that prove you aren't smart enough now? Look at your assessments and ask, "What would someone else see?" Keep looking for the bare facts, and try to stay with them for a few moments just as they are.

- *How is this interpretation serving me?*

Does this interpretation give you energy? Does it expand your possibilities? Does it bring you closer to what you most care about? Does it align with your values? Important note: it can be very easy to criticize yourself at this juncture. "I should have only loving interpretations." That is utter bullshit. Do not waste your time going down that road — the point is not to judge how you are interpreting your experiences but simply to notice. The thought that you should have only loving interpretations is just another interpretation, which can prompt you to ask, "How is this interpretation serving me?"

- *What are a few of my lifetime "this-is-just-the-way-I-am" or "this-is-just-the-way-it-is" statements?*

"This is just the way I am," declares Mary, as she reaches for her third double latte of the day. "I'm a high-powered person, and I need high-octane fuel." "My husband refuses to understand that I need him to demonstrate his affection with gifts. That's just what I need." Here are some more examples of these kinds of statements:

- I'm not smart enough to do what I want in life.
- I have to work really hard to get ahead.
- I'm too fat to be attractive to a partner.
- It's dangerous to reveal my true self to others; they will betray me more often than not.
- To be successful in business, you have to be a bitch. So if I'm successful, my husband and children will hate me, and I'll end up alone, and none of the hard work will be worth it, so why start?

- *Given the facts I have found, what interpretation can I create now?*

Is there a new story, grounded in these facts, that you might be willing to try on? "It's true that I flunked algebra. I was afraid of math; I was madly in love, and I had just discovered beer. In other words, I was eighteen. It's a wonder I passed English, and that's my best subject. Besides, I couldn't imagine why I would ever need to know algebra. Now that I am passionate about becoming a clinical social worker, I'll do whatever it takes to pass algebra, and that includes hiring a tutor."

It's Time to Swim

Jump in, the water is fine — by which I mean give one of the ideas in this chapter a try. Start right now: take a full breath and let it out with a sigh; put your attention and your hand on your heart and invite a memory or feeling of when you were beginning something deliciously wonderful, something that turned out to be incredibly, delightfully helpful; ask your heart a question like "Where do I want to begin?" Trust that one beginning step will be revealed because you are listening. Now take that step, no matter how small or insignificant it feels.

You already know how to do this. Set your computer or watch to remind you to check in with yourself, using the five steps. Or if that makes you rebel, decide for one week that every time you feel stressed, you'll connect with your heart and a memory of being at peace. Or read on and begin to create your Life Planner. My dearest wish is that you simply begin!

Mood Shifter

— ∞ —

Moods, more often than not, rule our lives, and sometimes these emotional highs and lows feel permanent, unchangeable. This handy mood index will remind you that no, your mood is not fixed — you can intervene and change it. Simply find the mood that rings the most true for you in the moment (you may want to pick more than one, but just start with one) and then go to the pages listed. You'll find exercises, questions, or stories that just may change your mind and your body — as well as your mood. Don't try to figure out why I listed certain page numbers for certain moods — there isn't a right answer. Let serendipity be your guide.

Comparing myself to others: 17, 22, 37, 58, 73, 100, 117, 140, 148, 169, 227, 239

Concerned about money: 22, 34, 54, 90, 98, 129, 143, 165, 176, 211

Confused about how to nurture myself: 5, 8, 9, 10, 12, 17, 22, 24, 31, 32, 34, 41, 46, 64, 78, 80, 92, 95, 107, 122, 177, 192, 237

Crabby: 17, 22, 41, 82, 95, 104, 122, 138, 145, 156, 162, 171, 182, 192, 220

Creative: 22, 37, 67, 69, 78, 82, 85, 97, 99, 113, 129, 139, 153, 162, 178, 190, 202, 222, 225

Depressed: 22, 31, 37, 41, 46, 53, 66, 74, 76, 94, 96, 105, 122, 132, 136, 138, 142, 147, 152, 175, 196, 209, 214, 220

Doing everything myself: 46, 51, 76, 84, 90, 95, 101, 124, 145, 177, 194, 231

Doing for others what I could be doing for myself: 67, 95, 96, 104, 152, 156, 162, 171, 188, 192

Eating for comfort: 16, 22, 37, 46, 51, 53, 64, 92, 96, 97, 107, 118, 127, 151, 173, 176, 199, 218

Energetic: 18, 46, 66, 69, 81, 114, 118, 138, 164, 174, 209, 216, 222

Exhausted: 10, 18, 22, 41, 46, 67, 82, 95, 97, 106, 118, 122, 161, 173, 182, 192

Facing a big challenge: 22, 31, 34, 46, 54, 66, 95, 123, 142, 177, 184, 190, 214, 235

Fearful, scared: 22, 34, 54, 64, 78, 86, 117, 128, 152, 156, 172, 184, 192, 202, 214, 229

Feeling like a failure: 21, 53, 72, 74, 107, 110, 153, 202

Feeling like everybody wants a piece of me: 46, 51, 57, 67, 101, 150, 160, 171, 194, 198

Fighting with a friend: 22, 53, 86, 107, 115, 133, 148, 197

Focused: 78, 84, 103, 140, 152, 154, 166, 208, 233, 235

Forlorn: 22, 37, 53, 76, 123, 138, 142, 169, 214

Frenzied: 1, 17, 22, 34, 46, 51, 67, 86, 96, 108, 115, 126, 130, 171, 172, 198

Frustrated: 22, 37, 57, 74, 83, 86, 90, 140, 149, 182, 192, 202

Grasping: 18, 21, 22, 37, 90, 95, 107, 112, 140, 145, 181, 190

Grateful: 34, 37, 66, 103, 113, 125, 130, 135, 154, 160, 187, 208, 219, 229

Grieving: 22, 53, 142, 175, 181, 185, 209

Guilty: 21, 22, 34, 37, 41, 53, 71, 73, 86, 138, 168, 173, 192

Having a fat-and-ugly attack: 17, 22, 37, 41, 53, 81, 84, 97, 119, 151, 187

Having an awful day: 12, 22, 37, 46, 53, 86, 112, 130, 132, 160, 171

Having lover/partner trouble: 22, 24, 53, 64, 107, 115, 133, 148, 197, 209

Ill: 16, 46, 51, 53, 86, 97, 114, 118, 141, 165, 169, 176, 186, 188, 192, 214, 229

Joyful: 37, 66, 92, 106, 112, 123, 137, 152, 154, 174, 190, 201

Judgmental: 21, 22, 24, 41, 53, 86, 112, 150, 169, 183, 205, 229

Lonely: 22, 37, 53, 85, 88, 96, 118, 121, 130, 137, 175, 200, 207, 210

Not sure what I'm feeling: 8, 18, 20, 22, 24, 34, 90, 105, 110, 115, 132, 151, 178, 201, 202, 240

Old, behind the times, sexless: 22, 53, 94, 164, 175

Overwhelmed: 2, 11, 18, 22, 30, 46, 53, 71, 72, 74, 76, 84, 86, 101, 103, 105, 120, 122, 130, 132, 145, 154, 161, 171, 182, 192, 208, 233

Pessimistic: 21, 22, 30, 53, 83, 86, 114, 119, 135, 160, 194, 214, 240

Playful: 18, 67, 69, 97, 114, 123, 161, 175, 191, 201, 206, 211

Powerless: 12, 22, 34, 41, 46, 51, 53, 88, 92, 132, 145, 148, 153, 160, 169, 189, 192, 202, 216, 222

Proud of myself: 34, 81, 110, 116, 178, 218, 222

Resentful: 21, 22, 51, 53, 114, 148, 150, 182, 194, 204, 229

Resigned: 22, 37, 41, 53, 76, 88, 95, 101, 110, 132, 145, 150, 160, 189, 192, 222, 240

Resisting: 13, 37, 66, 74, 78, 116, 120, 171, 172, 184, 200, 219

Sad: 22, 53, 112, 160, 204, 210

Sexy, lustful, passionate: 37, 83, 92, 114, 121, 133, 200, 207, 212

Spiritually longing: 3, 13, 22, 24, 29, 66, 74, 78, 103, 106, 113, 116, 172, 174, 181, 194, 210, 220, 227

Stuck, blocked: 5, 22, 24, 29, 34, 41, 46, 63, 72, 76, 90, 107, 110, 113, 132, 145, 150, 152, 192, 202, 219, 229, 223

Thinking unclearly: 13, 22, 24, 32, 64, 74, 92, 119, 130, 132, 145, 172, 208, 216

Unsupported: 17, 22, 29, 32, 34, 57, 66, 88, 90, 101, 132, 136, 181, 183, 194, 216, 231, 235

Worried: 22, 34, 53, 66, 73, 81, 88, 90, 116, 130, 138, 152, 181, 184, 210

Stories for Along the Way

On a good day, creating and organizing your life in this improv way feels natural and even easy. Things flow. Then your parents come to visit, you have a fight with your partner, you catch a cold, and there's a horrific deadline at work...and life organizing is out the window because you just don't have the time or energy, or it's too new a habit to rely on when you're under such stress. When these weeks and even months of self-forgetfulness and of falling back on simply willing life to happen befall me, it helps tremendously to read about how other women improvise their lives. What works for them? Below and throughout the rest of the book I share the stories of clients, retreat participants, and readers who have sent me accounts of how they create their lives. Many use the Life Planner, and some don't — and that's important, since this book and the five steps and six concepts are just a starting place, an outline to use as you articulate your own way. This is not the only way!

As you read these women's stories, imagine yourself surrounded by a circle of women, all sharing their stories. Notice which of their ideas or words spark curiosity or yearning in your heart. Sniff at that curiosity. Follow it. See what it wants you to experience in your ever-evolving spiral of life improvisation.

Stories for Along the Way: Amy's Three Questions

There's no shortage of top-ten lists of leafy vegetables, beauty products, affirmations, and herbal supplements that are guaranteed to make me feel better, happier, healthier. All these lists can make me feel like a recipe with a missing ingredient. What will make everything fall into place? What are the five or seven or ten things I need to do to be happy every day? Of course, life is not that simple! And yet it is, when I can quiet my monkey mind and the expectations and the desire to do everything right and just listen. I do this by asking myself three questions. The first is, *"What is my relationship with my feelings?"* Am I ignoring them, wallowing in them, defining myself by them, judging them, eating them away, sleeping them away, shushing them because they are too intense? This question gives me permission to feel whatever I'm feeling, with no fear of being labeled wrong or crazy, and with no need to ask why. Feeling, really feeling, allows flow and brings me back to center. Often I move my body. Have you ever tried to feel your anger or your pain or even your joy by sitting still? Instead of holding on to my feelings and storing them in my neck and lower back and the pit of my stomach, I let them flow, which feels oh, so much better. I know then that I am defined not by one feeling, no matter how dark or scary, but by a lifetime woven of a million colorful threads.

My next question is *"What is my relationship with God — or Spirit or Big Love or whatever I feel like calling the mysterious life force?"* Am

I connected, am I asking for help, am I turning over what's not mine, am I honoring the mysteries, miracles, and blessings in my life? A friend and I have a shorter version of this question, which is, "Where the *&%^ is my gratitude?" When I'm feeling grinchy or stuck, it can be so difficult to see the bigger picture and to remember how holding things lightly allows joy to flow. How overwhelming it would be to think we were running the show with no room for the unknown. How freeing to feel that we are here not just for ourselves but for a bigger purpose, to be of service: to life, to those we love, to those in need, to the planet. When I lose my connection to a power greater than myself, I can get lost in my own minitragedies and fear. When I reestablish that connection, it renews my sense of peace and trust and flow.

The third question is, *"What is my relationship with myself?"* Am I supporting and loving myself? Am I taking care of my needs? Not just my needs for steaming hot black tea with soy milk, the occasional yoga class, and a new pair of chocolate brown boots, but my *emotional* needs: my fierce need to be alone, my need to feel loved, my need to feel desired, my need to feel heard and understood, my need simply to have needs and express them. I was once horrified to be told I "lacked a relationship with self." I didn't know that was possible. But when I was asked how I took care of my emotional needs and didn't have an answer (didn't even know what emotional needs were), I realized I had some exploring to do: of my own inner nooks and crannies, my own strengths and weaknesses, my own blind spots, my own accountability, and mostly my own desires. When I choose to ask myself these three questions instead of thrashing around bemoaning my stuckness or my perceived flaws, I end up choosing life.

Stories for Along the Way: Michele's Marching Orders

I feel I have been given certain marching orders for my life, and these are encoded in the language of my desires. What I love and am attracted to shows me what I need to do next, where I need to go, whom I need to serve or connect with. These marching orders are present in the people I meet, the requests I get, the projects I'm drawn to work on. I'm always getting data about what to do and being guided by God.

In the morning, I wake up, I go to my studio, and I look at my day. Here is what I see: my husband needs help with something, I have four clients, and the laundry needs to be done. Then I look into my heart and ask myself, "What do I want today? What do I want today to feel like?" This is a softening, a listening to what I'm hungry for.

Then I say to God, "Here are these things on my list that people need from me and the things I need to get done, and here is what I yearn for. I walk through it with Spirit; we create together." I might pray, "Help this project succeed; make sure it is a blessing for everyone." I delegate to God, and then things don't weigh on me.

If I'm feeling overwhelmed about my day, I ask, "What is that a hunger for?" Or if I'm not looking forward to a particular conversation, I ask, "What can I do about that?" If I think I will need time to myself later in the day, I ask, "How will that happen?" This is where the marching orders come in — I have this big plan for my life, and I have to keep my radio on. I have to keep listening.

Creating Your Life Planner

*M*ost Life Planner users create their own planner — whether in a notebook, computer file, sketchbook, or even Photoshop. Or you can write in the weekly Life Planner pages of this book, which begin on page 80 or download the questions at my website to print and create your own notebook: jenniferlouden/lifeorganizer. We also offer a free app! Even if you choose to make your own planner, you'll want to use the various tools provided on the Life Planner pages. First off is intention; at the top of each week's spread, you'll notice a place to write your intention for the week. See Intention (p. 32) for reminders on how to do this. Next you'll see circles labeled "Let Go of," "Have to," and "Could do." You may find yourself writing the most important items within the circles and then, on a daily basis, using these labels in a three-column approach to structure your to-do list. Next come the mindful questions — which, as you know, are not about finding answers but opening up new ways of seeing and feeling. At the bottom of each spread, there is room for any notes you want to record for each day of the week.

When deciding what form to use, choose what you'll actually use. If, for example, writing in this book makes you feel cramped, you won't do it. If you hate to write, don't make yourself write; instead, paint, sketch, or talk out your responses. If you hate to do the same thing every day (I do), then don't! Nona, a user of an earlier version of the Planner, wrote, "Last year I rarely used my Life Planner because I put it in a large three-ring binder, and I never wanted to drag it around with me. If it's not where I am when I have free time, it isn't going to be used. I was also into making my Life Planner 'pretty.' I was so worried about jazzing it up that I never thought about making it practical. Once I made it practical, I used it."

Sample the ideas and stories below, and notice what sparks you to create your own sourcebook. And be sure to check out the passel of support tools at lifeorganizerbook.com.

Ideas for Your Planner

- Buy a spiral notebook in a size that you like (small if want to carry the Life Planner with you, large if you like to write big and a lot). When you record your responses to mindful questions, date the page.

Karen's Life Planner

- Play with where you store your notebook — by your bed for morning or evening review; with your calendar, datebook, or cell phone; in the car; in a bag with other "centering items" like meditation CDs, a small book of poetry, a bottle of essential oil; or in your sacred space where you center yourself and create.

- "I have done *Artist's Way* morning pages for years," Patti told me. (Julia Cameron, in her book *The Artist's Way*, created the practice of writing three pages longhand every morning about anything one wishes.) "Now what I do is one or two pages of morning pages, to clear the noise in my head. Then I spend a few moments breathing and calling in guidance. I turn to a question for that day. You see, I work my way through a week of questions day by day, sometimes doing one, sometimes two or three, and often repeating them several days in a row. I'm astonished by the insights I get, and the things I remember are most important to focus on. Then I check my computer calendar and make a to-do list that reflects what I learned. I'm very careful to date my journal pages, and I keep my life insights on Post-it notes, on my computer wallpaper, and on pieces of paper I hide in odd places, like the back of the fridge or in the shoes that I only wear when presenting to the bigwigs at work."

- Copy your favorite questions on sturdy paper, and put them in a container. Draw one or more questions randomly, then record your responses.

- Poppy creates digital scrapbook pages in Photoshop and then posts them to a separate blog as a way of keeping them gathered in the same place. (You can see some of her postings on the example pages.) Micki keeps hers on a "sister blog." She's part of a group of women who live all over the world and who meet over a phone bridge once a month; each woman also posts to their shared blog. They use the

Poppy's Life Planner

Life Planner questions as a way to focus their lives and their support for each other. They all post their responses, then offer ideas or thoughts or pats on the back, as needed. "We have a midnight Sunday deadline to get our responses up. The pressure and the sharing really work to keep us faithful, and it's brilliant what it does for our follow-through. It's also tremendously helpful to see how others are asking too much of themselves or committing too much to others."

- Helga was struggling with "keeping up." "I use my Life Planner as often as possible — and if I miss some weeks, then so be it. Sometimes I have the time to work with it but don't feel like doing it, and I don't feel guilty. That is key for me — no guilt. And instead of cutting or pasting or adding art, I use colored pens. I choose a color according to how I feel that day. Giving myself permission to start (and miss) the Life Planner in whatever way works for

Helga's Life Planner

me in the moment did me a world of good! Overcoming my inner perfectionist has reverberated into other areas of my life, gifting me with new freedom to 'be.' Breaking an old pattern in one area can have such lovely consequences elsewhere!"

- Lynn, a graphic artist in Santa Barbara, constructed a card deck out of the questions using a set of oversized kids' playing cards. On one side she pasted images from magazines, junk mail, and her own snapshots that seemed to "go with" the different questions on an intuitive level. "I think of this as my very own divination system. I draw a question card, or two. I might hold them and ask for help. I might stare at the image and see what it sparks in me."

- I use the Life Organizer app because it pings me and reminds me to check-in.

When? How Long? How Often?

The amount of time you spend with your Life Planner is, of course, highly personal, frequently changing, and always driven by what serves you best. It would be far too ironic to make the Life Planner into a should. That being said, it is a really good idea to focus a bit on when you'll be most likely to use the Planner. Otherwise it's too easy to create unrealistic or inflated expectations. It's far better to follow when you are naturally drawn to reflecting on your week or when you can sneak away for a bit of peace and quiet, or when you will be at home with some discretionary time on your hands. Study yourself and work with who you are

DESIRES

To increase my ability to receive
To remember that the Divine is my energy source
To exercise with joy five times a week
To weigh 124 pounds
To spend the right amount of time with Dad and Mom
To deepen my art making and be satisfied with the direction
To easily find the perfect sofa slip cover
To rewrite my novel
To find a way to be of service as a family
To play each day
To communicate with people I work with more clearly
To be outdoors more

Jennifer's Life Planner

— never use your Life Planner to push yourself into being someone you are not. Please!

"On Sunday nights I fill in answers to the weekly questions, as well as to the have-tos/could-dos/let-go-ofs," writes Suzie. "During the week, I jot down memorable things that happened that day that relate to the questions. This gets me to glance at my answers and remind myself of what I'm focusing on. It's how I recenter before I go to sleep, and it also helps me start the day thinking in terms of positive intentions!"

Poppy reports, "If I had to complete the week's worth of questions before I could move forward, I'd never catch up. Of course, I don't have to finish them. I can come back to a set of questions whenever I want, as long as I do it lovingly instead of forcing myself into it."

I do my organizer on Sunday nights or Monday mornings. When two weeks go by and I realize I have not used the questions, I take this as a sign that I'm neglecting my center and focusing too much "out there," that the expectations I have of myself are unrealistic, or that I'm making the questions into too big of a deal.

Janice looks at hers during her lunch hour, adding ideas and reading over what she wrote. "It only takes a minute or two, and it always sparks me to remember what kind of life I'm creating right in the moment."

If you notice yourself saying, "I should use my Life Planner," instead try asking yourself, "What do I want? What might I enjoy?" Shoulds, have-tos, and musts rob you of connection to desire and rob this process of its beauty.

Intervene in the rush of your daily life by setting a mindfulness prompt to go off at regular intervals. I use the Life Organizer app or the alarm on my phone. You could also use going to the bathroom, drinking water, or hanging up the phone as your cue to check in.

A number of women carry a question or two with them on index cards, and when they look at these questions, they are reminded to engage with their inner knowing. The point of this process is not to create some intricate ritual and complicated journal or date book — it is to point you inside and to give you some form to help you listen, record, and remember.

Some Simple Ideas

Remembering to use the Life Planner can be a challenge, so plan now how you'll work it into your life, how you will make it part of your daily round. You might:

- Put the book where you can see it.

- Make it part of your business or work planner.

- Put reminders in your work planner or computer calendar. That might mean that every Friday for one month your calendar to-do list says, "Life Planner."

- Decorate five Post-it notes that say, "I'm living inside out" or some other funky reminder, and put them on your bathroom mirror, inside your car, in your checkbook or wallet, or on the coffeemaker, where you will see them every day.

- Try using your Life Planner in the bathtub or in bed at night — or any time when you are especially relaxed.

- Ask a friend to email you a reminder once a week.

- Do it with a group. I put free groups together via my email list. Join at jenniferlouden.com/lifeorganizer.

- Most of all, connect with your heart, and let when and how often you use the Planner spring only from there!

The Life Planner

*Fifty-two Weeks of
Mindful Living*

1–4

How do we create a life carved from our deepest knowing? How do we live a life of our making?

We become curious apprentices of our own lives, willing to keep our eyes open to ourselves, even when we would rather shrink away in disgust or hide behind fear.

We listen to the twitch in our back, the pang in our stomach, the depth charge of our headache, the cold we get every time we visit our parents.

We offer ourselves, and ask from others, the sacrament of forgiveness.

We ask, "What would I be willing to die for?"

We become miracle detectives.

For every complaint we launch into the world, we counter it with an action of gratitude.

We dip into our days and let them run through us, refusing to sip the sweet from a thimble and gulp the sour from a bucket.

We recount all the ways one person can make a difference in the world, and then we stake our claim to making our difference.

To paraphrase poet Derek Walcott, we feast on our life and give our heart back to ourselves.

We read poetry and dance to ecstatic music when we feel the urge to gobble cookies and watch bad TV.

We accept that straying from the path is always part of the journey. We ask, "What would I do if I didn't care if I failed?"

What if your most sacred mission each day were to take impeccable care of yourself? "Comfort did not always have its present 'soft' connotations of physical ease, contentment, and well-being," notes John Ayto in *The Dictionary of Word Origins*. It originally meant "to make someone stronger." When I think about all the things we are called to do simply to survive, let alone thrive, I see strength as one of the qualities we need most.

It is intriguing that in the Christian tradition, the Holy Spirit is also called the Comforter and that this aspect of God guides followers "in the way of the truth." Comfort and truth go together: we need to strengthen ourselves and be kind to ourselves so that we can follow our truth.

As you venture into your first round of life organizing, try on an attitude of "How can this serve me and help me be a conduit for creative love?" instead of "I should do this because it's good for me." Consider your Life Planner a place of pleasure, a temple where you connect with life.

Stories for Along the Way: Willow Sings Her Soul

When I was twenty-one, I came face-to-face with the irrefutable truth that to live the life of my soul, I would need to sing it into existence. Literally. From that day forward, I committed myself to a path where song leads. I have learned, through repeated, stubborn attempts to turn away from this truth, that the path carved by song is simply who I am. As Martha Graham so wisely counseled, it is not my business to judge my gifts, but to make use of them. This has not been an *easy* way. But for me, it has been the *only* way through. In the landscape of my life, song is the bridge that yokes body, mind, soul, and spirit.

To find the breath for this path, I must tend the temple of this body. To tap the wisdom, I must clear the obscurations in my mind. To receive the force of yearning and longing, I must be willing to feel the 360-degree curvature of my heart's rhythmic pulsation, through all its textures of emotion. To ground the light of Spirit, I must surrender to a source greater than my small self. Music requires all of me. Recognizing and embracing music as the anchor of my life makes all else possible. It is the difference between living *my* life and living someone else's unlived life — which, as we all know, requires a lot of disembodied gymnastics that leave one hollow at heart.

It has taken me three and a half decades to discern my own rhythm on the planet, and to respect what my body, mind, soul, and spirit need to live according to the laws of love — that is to say, love for myself and love for others, which are, ultimately, indivisible. I have sought mentors who radiate this capacity; I have drawn on the inspiration of living exemplars of the path less often taken. What most allows me to compose a life worth living is remembering to cultivate joyful effort and patience. Focusing on learning to give and receive love through all my exchanges with the world puts everything in its rightful perspective. To court this Love with a true joy for the enterprise itself, regardless of the outcome, is paramount. It took me three and a half decades to understand what I am not, and to focus on that which my soul is naturally drawn to. To allow for the death of ideas about who I 'should' be, and what I 'should' do. To allow room for my love affair with the Divine to outshine, and shine into, every other aspect of my life. To arrive at a place where my most urgent, daily call to the universe is this: Please show me how to give and receive love.

Of course, losing sight of this clarity, and reframing it, is a daily practice. Courting empathetic joy — the ability to take pleasure and delight in others' successes — helps tremendously. Asking for help is always a victory! Recognizing the power I have to share with and support others, even when I feel less than well equipped to do so, always refocuses my view. Practicing the art of gratitude, especially when I am feeling miserly and contracted, is an enactment of faith itself. Dedicating whatever benefit may arise from my day-to-day efforts helps me to feel the interconnection between us all. This is how I sing my soul into being, breath by breath.

Let go of

What experience or feeling do I yearn for today?

Give yourself the blessing of stopping and listening, noticing what you truly want. Let it be heard, no matter how outrageous or inconsequential it may seem. Then make time today for at least a taste of your yearning — if you yearn to take the day off, take lunch away from your desk. If you yearn to sleep for a week, go to bed early. If you yearn to love a romantic partner, love those around you. This yearning can become your intention for the week.

How might shadow comforts or time monsters block me from trusting myself or from exploring the yearning I just named?

Shadow comforts or time monsters take your time and energy, and they also sow the suspicion that you aren't capable or trustworthy enough to create a life through being kind to yourself.

sunday	*monday*	*tuesday*

dates

_____

Faith is not a commodity we either have or don't have — it is an inner quality that unfolds as we learn to trust our own deepest experience.

— **Sharon Salzberg**, *Faith*

Have to

What would help my body feel listened to and loved?
Some answers might be: a farm-fresh salad, a trance-dance class, a rainwater shower, a Shiatsu massage, not beating yourself up because you couldn't zip your pants.

How have I been talking to myself lately?
Is your interior dialogue one of kindness, or are you brandishing the whip? When the whip comes down, focus on speaking to yourself like your best friend would.

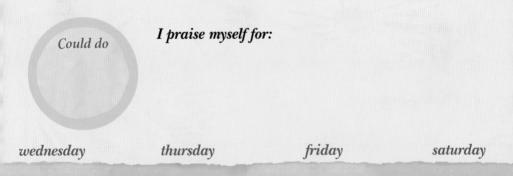

Could do

I praise myself for:

wednesday   *thursday*   *friday*   *saturday*

Let go of

What am I most passionate about this week?

Name one desire this week, and see what wants to make love to the world through you. If you don't feel passionate about anything, then ask yourself, "What would I turn off the TV for? What attracts my attention even a little?" These questions may point you to your intention.

What or who do I want to say no to this week?

In what situations could saying no enhance your happiness or lead to more time and energy for you? Building your "no muscle" helps you increase self-trust.

What or who do I want to say yes to?

Grant yourself permission to open your arms to what beckons, to what you want.

sunday	monday	tuesday

dates

_____

Decide daily to be the agent of your own life —
you have nothing to lose and so much to gain.

Have to

What touch, texture, or physical contact would nourish and calm me?

Some answers might be: using towels warm from the dryer, snuggling with your dog or cat, putting an old tennis ball under your body and relaxing into the pressure of where your body meets the ball...

What might shift if I used the interruptions of my life this week to come into the present moment?

Interruptions are never going away. What would shift if you accepted them as an opportunity to be aware of the flow of life, the moment, the gift of breath?

Could do

I trust:

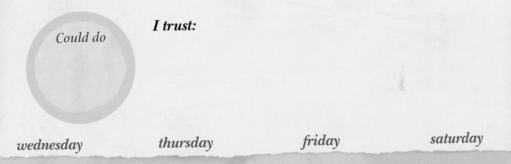

wednesday   thursday   friday   saturday

Let go of

What do I want to learn in the coming months?

Would you like to speak Spanish, to accept your partner, to receive as much you give, to be more present? Your life insight list may give you some ideas.

What do I need to dump out of my brain to make more space for what I would rather focus on?

We can handle only four to six life focuses at one time — any more than that, and we get frazzled. These focuses can change often. For one three-month period, they might be: helping your child with college submissions, completing a big project at work, knitting, and getting exercise. In the next four months, they might be: planning a vacation, hiring a new assistant, connecting with your partner, and eating in a new way. Choose your four to six life focuses, date them, and write them someplace prominent in your Planner — maybe near your life insights. You may find relating your weekly intentions to your life focuses helpful.

sunday   *monday*   *tuesday*

dates

_____

*Knowing happens only in the present moment —
delusion, worry, and conjecture happen
only in the future.*

Have to

***Creative self, what enchantment and soul food are
you hungry for? I'm willing to listen.***
Some answers might be: visiting a fabric store or one of
those "lifestyle" stores where you look at everything but
don't buy a thing.

With whom might I share my idea of comfort this week?

Could do

I'm satisfied with:

wednesday   thursday   friday   saturday

Let go of

What recent mistakes can now be turned into compost, and what new beginning will I grow in this compost?
If this question stumps you, list your recent errors on the left-hand side of a piece of paper, and on the right-hand side write a possible opportunity to create or grow something new.

What is my biggest source of stress, irritation, or annoyance these days?
Record one person, situation, or upcoming event.

What story am I telling myself about this stressor?
Record everything you have been saying to yourself. Keep your hand moving, don't edit or censor, and write for three minutes (or longer if it feels right).

| *sunday* | *monday* | *tuesday* |

dates

_____

Success has more to do with the learner you are than with the expert you have become. Success thrives on the compost of your errors.

— Molly Gordon, author and master coach

Have to

What are the facts in what I just wrote?

Underline the facts in what you just wrote — something you could prove to another person, like "It's 48 degrees outside" or "My eyes are blue" *not* "It's cold in here" or "My eyes are tired and droopy."

Given these facts, what might I be open to doing or feeling today that I haven't done or felt before?

If you had only these facts to go on, what might you be inclined to believe, see, and do? Tune in to your new possibilities.

Could do

I'm ready to receive:

wednesday   thursday   friday   saturday

5–8

East of Ordinary
There exists the landscape where
you take yourself by the hand.
Where you walk forward trembling with tears
running down your face,

West of Doubt
where you fear your greatness and
embrace it anyway.
We join hands and
listen for the whispers of how we each make a
difference.

North of Hello
we gather
the courage
for the doing.

South of Regret
we loosen our jaws, lean our shoulders away
from our ears,

let our eyes turn upwards.
It need not be hard,
we have each other.

Trust. Without it, it's very challenging to live in this creative, desiring heart and spirit–guided way we're exploring here. It makes everything so much easier when you can trust what you desire, when you can trust your deepest experiences, when you can trust yourself to stay connected and aware, when you can trust that when you do disconnect, you'll connect again soon.

How the hell do you do that? By being aware of what you do trust about yourself. Aware that at the times when you listened to your desires, when you listened to your heart first, your life, your well-being, your bank account did not go down the toilet. As one client said to me, "The more I do what I truly want and the more I genuinely appreciate what I have, especially opportunities and relationships, the more miracles happen."

When we forget to gently pay attention to what works, to celebrate the 1001 things that we do that are good and easy and beneficial, and instead pay attention to the two things that go wrong or disappoint us, we spin off into being a victim or judging ourselves. We lose touch with the what is good and whole now.

Trust, then, is born out of paying attention, day-by-day, moment-by-moment, to what is actually happening and then surrendering to that. With a little practice, you begin to notice that you are okay in this moment; you begin to trust that you are okay. You begin to trust yourself to listen for your next step, and then you ask yourself, "Did that work? Am I okay?" which breeds the confidence and trust to continue. *It is that simple.*

Stories for Along the Way: Molly's Fog Bank

In 1996, when my coaching practice was brand-new, I went through a time that I came to call "the Fog Bank." So much was unknown to me at that time, and, in retrospect, I notice that many (all?) of the unknowns were "shoulds": How should I market myself? What kind of coach should I be? Should I enroll in a training program? Whom should I trust? Should I be trying harder to find clients? One of my favorites went something like this: "Shouldn't I be more worried?"

That particular "should" made me aware of the fog bank. I recall standing at the drawing table in my office/studio, gazing south toward the Bainbridge ferry terminal, drinking in the unseasonably bright sun, and musing about all the questions before me and how disinclined I was to worry. An image formed, more in bodily awareness than in visual cues. I felt myself in a dense fog bank, standing somewhere near the edge of a cliff overlooking the sea. I felt utterly safe. The fog was an enfolding blanket. It warmed and grounded me. I had the thought, "But how can I see where I am going?"

The answer was immediate: "I can see as far as my outstretched hand. I can feel whether the ground is firm or treacherous through my feet. I always have enough information to take one step."

That time remains in my memory as one of peculiar grace. I walked in that fog bank for several months, cozy, protected, and gifted with what, for me, was one of the sweetest and most unexpected blessings: a perfect sense of pacing. In keeping a measured and deliberate pace that did not conflict with the quality or quantity of guidance I received, I noticed that uncertainty did not need to produce suffering.

One of the hallmarks of this period was spending hours each day in activities that were not "productive." I exercised, meditated, and wrote. I was studying singing at the time, and I would practice for an hour every day. I took time to walk to the bank and the post office, and I prepared meals for myself. I came to regard the four or five hours devoted to these activities as my most important overhead expenses.

Eventually, I came out of the fog bank, and many of those practices diminished over time. Sometimes I'm sad about that, imagining that if only I had kept them up I would be, well, damn near perfect. But the truth is that I don't believe in holding on to practices beyond their natural life. I'm more interested in learning how to recognize and attend to the new practices that want to emerge whenever I experience a significant shift.

Intention:

Let go of

How is confusion or not knowing showing up in my life these days? What might be the gift or opportunity in these moments of not knowing?
You may have to reflect on this question a few times this week.

What do I desire this week? What calls to me, even if it doesn't make logical sense or I'm certain I don't have the time or energy?
If you have been very busy or pushing yourself, you may need to take this question with you on a walk or in the bath, so that you will feel soothed enough to listen.

What are the three or four things I think about most?
Record what runs through your mind most often.

sunday   *monday*   *tuesday*

dates

_____

Cultivate grace through self-compassion.

Have to

Is this what I want to think about?
Notice your thoughts. Are you believing them?

What do I want to receive into my life this week? What gifts offered to me by the bountiful universe am I ready to accept?
Notice whether you are resentful of giving to others, and if you have been giving anything you want to ask for or give to yourself.

Could do

I've always wanted to:

wednesday   *thursday*   *friday*   *saturday*

Intention:

Let go of

If I could do or be or feel anything this week, what would it be?

Some possible ideas: wild, spontaneous, organized, decluttered, in love with your body, grateful, content...

Am I willing to take one doable step toward what I want?
Decide yes or no but do decide.

What one basic need do I want to pay attention to this week?
Check in with the minimum requirements that you created back in What Is Life Organizing? (p. 46).

sunday   **monday**   **tuesday**

dates

_____

Unearth hope that's as wide as the prairie sky.

Have to

How and to where can I slip away for a mini-retreat really soon?
Tonight after the report is done or the kids are in bed, tomorrow at lunch, Saturday morning instead of running errands...at the library, between fresh sheets, under a blanket on the couch, with a close friend...

When I think of a current favorite shadow comfort or time monster (like _____ or _____) I think I could actually be hungry for _____.

Could do

I know:

wednesday   thursday   friday   saturday

Intention:

Let go of

What could I lean back on and trust today?
It may be a memory or a feeling of being loved; it may be your felt sense of Spirit; it may be your love of a person or place.

What am I too busy to think about?
What might you take the time to gently name just to give it breathing room?

What is not thinking about this costing me?
Name the price.

sunday   monday   tuesday

dates

_____

Melt into the echo of your heart, cradle yourself in the belly of this moment, with bliss warming you, urging you to love the dark as much as the light.

Have to

What physical activity would I like to enjoy this week?

Just for this week.

What do I want to enjoy this season that I haven't yet made time for?

Allow this season's truest pleasures to help you slow down and savor your life.

Could do

I tolerate:

wednesday   thursday   friday   saturday

Let go of

What is one way I'd love to flow with my life today?
Let yourself feel into the flow first; move, stretch, recall a heart memory of being in flow with your life force. Then jot down the first ideas that surface, and commit to one.

I could invite more rest and quiet into my life this week by . . .
Some answers could be: dropping repetitive worrying thoughts, buying a new pillow, taking a warm bath with lavender and lemongrass, letting go of what is not yours to carry…

sunday   *monday*   *tuesday*

dates

_____

Desire is the movement of life that carries us where we yearn to be.

Have to

What emotional release do I need, if any? Is anything, no matter how trivial, clogging my emotional arteries?

Staying current with your emotions takes courage, self-compassion, and, often, time. It might be easier to watch TV or to work late, but the price you pay for avoiding or denying your emotions is far too high.

Body, what intuitive messages are you sending me? I'm ready to listen.

Write whatever comes to mind. Often the more out of character your response, the more valuable it is.

Could do

I respect:

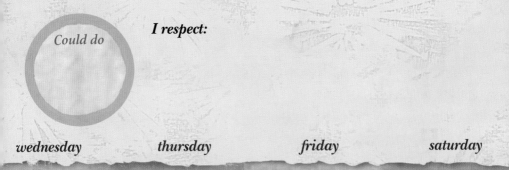

wednesday   thursday   friday   saturday

9–12

"Being ordinary and being nobody aren't the same thing," my friend says to me when I try to explain my struggle over needing to feel special.

My friend Mary writes a story about a woman whose husband has passed away and whose daughters are begging her to get busy. "You need to do things, Mom," one daughter insists. But she doesn't understand. Can't they see how busy she is? Someone has to watch the apples bud on the old tree. Someone has to notice the peach-colored light as it travels across the oak floor. Someone has to walk outside in the early-morning dew and taste one blueberry to see if its moment of precise, firm sweetness has arrived.

In his acceptance speech for the Nobel Prize in Literature, Pablo Neruda said, "I have often maintained that the best poet is he who prepares our daily bread: the nearest baker who does not imagine himself to be a god. He does his majestic and unpretentious work of kneading the dough, consigning it to the oven, baking it in golden colors and handing us our daily bread as a duty of fellowship. And, if the poet succeeds in achieving this simple consciousness, this too will be transformed into an element in an immense activity."

If you want to write the poem that sears itself on the heart or open a bakery whose goods make the taste buds sprout wings or give birth to a movement, and you do these things to prove that you are special, no matter what you accomplish, it will never be enough. Those accomplishments will fall through your fingers like air, even as they nourish the rest of us.

If you want to write the book or open the bakery or birth the movement because you are drawn to do these things through your desire to make love to life, then your hands will be brimming and you will be nourished. And by nourishing yourself in this way, you will be a light in the world.

Stories for Along the Way:
Elaine Superwoman Fades Away

I grew up in the era of Gloria Steinem, women's lib, the ERA, Helen Reddy's "I Am Woman," and Helen Gurley Brown's *Cosmo*. At eighteen, I had no dreams of marriage, children, and a picket fence around a cookie-cutter suburban house. Instead I envisioned business suits, practical pumps, and alligator bags in my future fighting the glass ceiling. Then, I found myself married, a mother, and cleaning a three-bedroom, two-bath house as well as working full-time in the corporate arena. I did it all. *All the time.* I saw it as my role. Working was what I always thought I would do — in an office being a clerk, a supervisor, a department head and at home rearing a child, cleaning, cooking, and doing laundry. None of that sitting at home playing with children and watching soap operas. My time was too important. I must be hardworking. I must be productive. I must be successful.

At thirty, I was getting married a second time, raising my child, managing a department, and attending college at night and on weekends. I was always in a blind rush but managing to get it all done — and done well, I might add.

At thirty-five, college degree and a teaching certificate in hand, I had a classroom to organize and orchestrate. I was responsible for teaching children to add, subtract, read, and write for the first time. I was still guiding my son through life, dealing with his father, dodging the slings and arrows of the teenage years. By this time I had no idea how I had gotten on my little hamster wheel or how I could get back off it. I was so busy I didn't realize I was losing my sanity, if I ever truly had it to begin with. The pace of life was breakneck, and I didn't have time to think about it.

I was forty-five, and my son had graduated from college and had taken off to pursue his dreams. I quit teaching and relocated to a new house in a new state with my husband, who was often away traveling. I was alone, and there was nothing I had to do, except think. That's when it hit me.

All the rules I lived by had been self-imposed, based on the "I should do it all" philosophy. I had lost any semblance of myself. So for almost eighteen months, I slept. It took that long before I could be calm and quiet enough to hear my own voice again. It started as a whisper that told me to simplify. I sold things, pitched things, sent things off to Goodwill. I simplified my finances. I simplified my expectations. I planted a garden, and I cooked real meals. But something was still missing.

I started listening more carefully. What I heard was a voice telling me that it was okay to do what I enjoyed. I wasn't wasting time. I wasn't being unproductive. I could build a life on my strengths and my passions. All of a sudden, my stress was gone. I quit worrying. I quit feeling I was responsible for everyone and everything. A funny thing happened. I found a new career. I wake up in the morning anxious to learn something new, to read something interesting, or to talk to someone who intrigues me. Then I take that information and create something with it. After thirty years, I feel such joy in the things I do.

My sanity is revived, or perhaps gained for the first time. I take things slower. I take time to listen to my own voice. Sanity is the result of listening to and trusting yourself to do the right thing for you. Perfection truly is in the eye of the beholder.

Stories for Along the Way: Sandi's Ritual

I have a ritual that soothes and comforts me more than anything: it consists of a pot of tea, a lit candle, a gratitude journal, and a morning prayer on my knees. Without this hour alone while I listen to my beloved snoring on the other side of the wall, I would not be a fit human being. I would not be awake to the tired and frazzled places in me that just need to be seen and heard. Because when I am tired and frazzled, what I'm most missing is my own attention. During this sacred hour each morning I remind myself to put down the sword of striving and pick up the light of acceptance. I remind myself that I do not need to change to be okay. What a relief!

Let go of

What do I need less of this week?
Some ideas: less self-doubt, less denial about your bank balance, fewer errands, less cooking, less shouting, less driving...

What could be a good rhythm for my week?
Check in with your body and your heart to see what feels right.

Am I doing something for someone else that I want to do for myself?
What might you be giving to others that you could claim for yourself? What might open up for you?

| *sunday* | *monday* | *tuesday* |

dates

_____

It is not your job to make the rain fall and the corn grow.
It is not your job to make everybody you love happy.
At some point, you have to realize you aren't God.

Have to

How can I shape my mood to support me in flowing with life this week?
Your moods are flexible and changeable. Moving your body, listening to or playing music, being in or near the water, and laughing are all simple ways to change a mood.

What are my current four to six life focuses? Have I been adding more "pots to the stove" than I have burners (i.e., time and energy)?

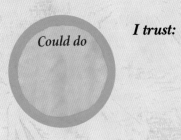

Could do

I trust:

wednesday   thursday   friday   saturday

Let go of

Spirit, what would you have me do, feel, or think to be fully alive this week?

You may want to use the five steps of connect, feel, inquire, allow, and accept to deepen this question.

What one thing could make my life more joyful this week? Lighter? Easier?

Some answers could be: buying a new garbage can with a lid that keeps the dog out; arranging dogwood branches in a vase; creating a shrine to your spirit; looking at a situation, habit, or relationship in a fresh way...

sunday   *monday*   *tuesday*

dates

To be ordinary is to be available for love.

Have to

What shadow comforts and time monsters suck me in these days?

When your boss yells at you, when your partner or child criticizes you, when your pants don't fit, what do you turn to for comfort?

What would I like to be free of this week?

Choose one thing — a feeling of being behind, beating yourself up for eating sugar, fear of losing your job. Every time this one thing arises this week, say something like this to yourself: "I'm taking a week off. I know you have a lot to teach me and I'm taking a rest this week."

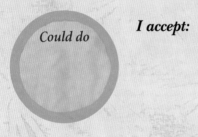

Could do

I accept:

| wednesday | thursday | friday | saturday |

Intention:

Let go of

If I knew now what I will know at the end of my life, what would I choose to do with my precious life energy this week?

Let the Wise Woman in you, the elder, your inner Grandmother, help you direct your choices this week. Invite her wisdom to speak to you right now.

What could my Wise Woman, my inner Grandmother, the self I will become, give me to help me create a week that fits me?

Ask Grandmother to answer this for you.

sunday	*monday*	*tuesday*

dates

_____

Be curious earlier.

— Ann Cheng, master coach

Have to

What small shifts can I make that might enhance my routine, give me a more grateful, flowing, God-smacked perspective?

Routines are unavoidable and often draining, especially those that involve parenting small children or caring for older parents. Consciously look for ways to make your routines lighter.

What hidden gift wants to unfurl in me this week?

Let this question percolate in your heart; try living the question rather than forcing a response.

Could do

I'm not ready to let go of:

wednesday   thursday   friday   saturday

Let go of

How do I feel about the choices I've been making in the past few weeks or months?
Reflect on what your choices have been.

Who am I becoming with these choices? Are these choices moving me toward or away from what I most value? Are they moving me away from or toward a life that fits me?

As I look back over my "Have to," "Could do," and "Let go of" lists since starting this process, what do they teach me about my life? Do I see any patterns? Am I willing to notice any small shifts that I have made?

sunday   *monday*   *tuesday*

dates

_____

Grant yourself buoyant freedom from shoulds and have-tos, since nothing clouds inner knowing as thoroughly as inner hectoring.

Have to

When have my shadow comforts been most active? What about my time monsters?

Name the triggers when you have found yourself drawn to these old friends. Can you name a time when they weren't shadow comforts or time monsters at all but instead actually gave you what you needed?

What gifts have my life insights brought? What has remembering them given me or saved me?

It might be helpful to look at your date book or journal to jog your memory of the past weeks or months.

Could do

I am grateful for:

wednesday   thursday   friday   saturday

13–16

Would a weight lift off my shoulders if I realized that it's normal to feel pulled between choices, that it's normal to want to do more than I have time or energy for, and that it's normal to have to choose between two equally wonderful things, that it's actually a sign I'm a fascinating, amazing person?

Would life become more pleasurable if I remembered that fear and doubt appear only when I project myself forward in time? What is here, right now? It's mine for the savoring. Would my heart grow twenty sizes larger if I decided that bullying myself was violence hiding under the guise of discipline, and that loving myself into my true shape is the path that will make me proudest?

Would I be more accepting of my rhythm if I saw myself in the tides? If I could feel my heart opening and closing, letting in and then retreating, giving me time to bring in and make mine what I have experienced? Would I be more loving with myself if I remembered that my rhythm is the rhythm of nature, of breath, of water, of learning, of life itself?

Would wonder be the prevailing mood of my life if

I could feel seahorse colonies dancing, penguins protecting their eggs, icebergs calving, wolves burrowing in their dens? If I could always see before me the cave paintings at Lascaux, Chagall's stained-glass windows in the Fraumünster Church in Zurich, Hetch Hetchy valley, a Two Grey Hills Navajo rug, babies in utero, the mind of someone I love, the Big Bang?

Stories for Along the Way: Dana's Prayer Cards

I keep a basket of images on my craft table, a well-worn container filled with the makings for a simple collage process I call Visual Prayer Cards. The idea is to create a spontaneous prayer in visual form. I have torn the images from the pages of magazines, old calendars, books, even junk mail. I also add color copies of favorite photos to the basket. I select the pictures based on the negative or positive charge they elicit. Nearby are a glue stick, scissors, and four-by-six-inch pieces of white card stock.

When I feel myself growing wobbly from all the "shoulds" and the "ought-tos," I play soft music, light a candle, and take a deep breath. Spending a few minutes of reflective time looking through my image basket to select pictures opens my heart to the present moment. I cut the images and glue them into place on a blank card to create my visual prayer. Words and phrases torn or cut from magazines are sometimes a helpful addition. I spend several minutes studying the story within the collage. Then I turn the card over and write my immediate thoughts and feelings, a poem, or a prayer. The entire process takes fifteen to twenty minutes. Time and time again, while creating a visual prayer, I have felt an internal shift from frustration or overwhelm to inspiration and calm. Crossing the bridge from *doing* to *being*, through the creation of visual prayers, brings me home again, to my center.

Intention:

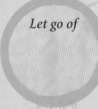

Let go of

What inspires me these days? How could I follow this inspiration, be shaped by its energy?
There is no one answer, just what arises in you now.

Body, what signals are you sending me that I need to pay attention to?
Some answers could be: tense shoulders, sugar cravings, swoops of creative energy, the need to be outdoors, a recurring dream, a reminder to get more sleep or to make a doctor's appointment…

What do I resent these days?
Let yourself be petty as you make this list. Then you might take one or two items and put them into this sentence: "Because _____ took _____ away from me, I can never _____." Yes, this is an exaggeration — and that lets you see what you feel you have lost.

sunday   *monday*   *tuesday*

dates

I was a hidden Treasure and I longed to be known,
so I created the creation to be known.

— Hadith Qudsi (Islamic holy saying)

Have to

What kind of self-nurturing would cultivate more
self-trust in me?
Hint: it is usually not shadow comforts.

How in touch with my heart have I been lately?
There is no right way; just a check-in reminder.

Could do

I forgive:

wednesday   *thursday*   *friday*   *saturday*

Let go of

How can I meet myself where I am today?

Practitioners in the healing professions, like therapy and coaching, learn to meet the client where she is, not where they want her to be or think she should be. What might shift for you if you approached today from a viewpoint of "This is where I am; what do I need?"

How can I connect deeply with something larger than me, larger than my needs, my agenda, my plans?

Some ideas: seeing love in a beloved's eyes, meditating, praying, watching waves...

sunday   *monday*   *tuesday*

dates

Be in devotional relationship to your life force.

— Shiva Rea, yoga teacher

Where or when do I find myself focusing outside of myself, on what others think of me?

In these moments, you can choose to breathe deeply and bring your focus inside by asking, "What do I want?"

If I want to, I can nurture myself in a way that celebrates the current season by:

Could do

I praise myself for:

wednesday   thursday   friday   saturday

Intention:

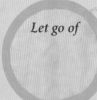

Let go of

If I created my week with my body as my ally, taking into consideration its needs, I might . . .

Body, what pleasure do you crave?
Ask your body — not your mind — what it desires. Notice if you automatically veto what it wants, deeming it too indulgent.

How can I connect with someone today in an honest, utterly "me" way?
Imagine how this connection will feel in your body. Let yourself feel how hungry for, and perhaps a little afraid of, this you are.

sunday   *monday*   *tuesday*

dates

_____

The body does not lie, but we sure can get
in the way of hearing its truth.

Have to

What simple practice could help me connect with my wholeness?
Victoria's practice is to remember what she's grateful for before she gets out of bed. I move my body without a plan, listening to where it wants to move. Naomi goes into her garden and feels the life growing there.

What media experiences do I choose to take in this week? What media experiences do I choose to let go of?
We are shaped and influenced by what we watch, read, and listen to.

Could do

I accept:

wednesday   *thursday*   *friday*   *saturday*

Intention:

Let go of

What I am most committed to these days?

What do your actions reveal about your commitments? What are you doing with your time these days? You may need to glance at your calendar if you get sleepy or fuzzy when considering this question. You may not want to know, so be gentle.

How am I fighting against or denying reality? Is this fight increasing my stress?

Thoughts like "I hate that this is happening" or "If we just had _____, then I wouldn't be in this mood" reveal reality. Try "I wish this wasn't happening, and it is," or "I wish we had _____, and we don't."

I've been honoring my minimum requirements lately by:

sunday   *monday*   *tuesday*

dates

_____

Delight in being a perpetual work in progress — is there a better choice?

Have to

What gift could I offer to someone this week?
Bringing in your neighbor's recycling bins, smiling at someone who is frowning in the grocery store, giving up your seat on the bus, shining out love during a meeting…

What inspiration am I hungry for?
Brainstorm at least ten outrageous, ultimate ideas (attend the Royal Theater in Madrid; go to opening night at Cannes; paint alongside your favorite artist) and then find the core of one to treat yourself to — like a painting outing with a good friend or attending the opera or renting a French film.

Could do

I know:

wednesday   *thursday*   *friday*   *saturday*

17–20

Ask a woman what she most craves, and most likely the answer won't be more money, a better body, or a house by the ocean; it will be time and rest. Genuine, fill-yourself-up-completely rest, which is, of course, related to time, since we rarely believe we have the time to rest. Yet without sufficient deep rest, we can't create anything of value, either because the noise in our heads is too loud or because we don't have the energy to follow through on our ideas and desires. Many a coaching client of mine heard a clarion call to redirect her life yet was unable to heed it because she had been neglecting her need for true rest for too long. The well wasn't just dry — she was going to have to drill a new one.

Yet rest does not recharge us if it is always an escape from life. I love watching a chick flick as much as the next woman, but if that's all I ever did for rest, I'd quickly become brittle and burned out. (I know — I've done it.) We need downtime, playtime, and we must have a connection to something bigger than ourselves if we are to recharge in the way that we are so fiercely hungry for.

What if, when we can't get the rest we crave, can't get to that territory where our minds slow and our shoulders drop away from our ears, it's because we aren't authentically connecting to Source? What if we are exhausted because we are trying to do everything alone, even to the point of believing we must create the very energy that animates our bodies and spirits? The Sufi spiritual tradition teaches that whatever you are most needy for is exactly what Source wants to give you. Your neediness is your invitation to ask for the quality you need — peace, love, tolerance, energy — to drink it in, to receive. Our inability to recharge is often because we have to stop, really stop, and feel into our cravings, our neediness, our lack, and allow those to be the portal. Are you willing to wait and willing to ask?

The more we truly live from our hearts, the more rest and self-nurturing and relaxation become a way of life — a satisfying texture of action and calm, expansion and contraction, giving and replenishing. Genuine rest becomes part of our lives not because we have to make time for it but because we are willing to be needy and ask for what we need from Spirit, because we are offering our gifts to the world with verve and integrity. Life, in other words, is no longer clutched in our tight fists. And that is truly restful.

Stories for Along the Way: Noelle Floats

I'd been building my practice as a life coach and SoulCollage® facilitator and had clients to see and workshops to market, and I was gearing up for a large exhibit. When I needed them the most, my energy and creativity were not there. I felt dried up. So I took six weeks off.

My mentor told me about her friend in the Mt. Rainier foothills who raises cattle. Every summer, when the grass is tall and plentiful, he has a natural break from his routine as the cows take care of themselves, roaming and grazing to their hearts' content. Every business has a season when it doesn't require full attention. I looked at my calendar; I had no workshops scheduled and only a sprinkling of coaching appointments. August was my slow time. The plan was simple — for the next six weeks I would play! I would do only those things absolutely necessary to keep my business running until September. The rest of the time was my own.

I chose an image to represent my playful intention, a picture from the 1940s of a party of men and women, dressed in their most festive attire, complete with frilly parasols, floating down a lazy river in inner tubes on a summer's day. This was what I was after: play without a goal, free-flowing like a river.

In the six weeks that followed, a natural structure evolved. I wrote morning pages after breakfast. I drew a SoulCollage card at the start of each week. I went to the beach as often as possible. I read all the Harry Potter novels for the first time. And as ideas for new creative projects began to emerge (as they will when we give ourselves the time and space just to be), I returned to the image that reflected my intention. Instead of my usual response to ideas — making plans and lists — I allowed my ideas to float down the river with me, each in its own inner tube, inviting them to play with me, writing them down to return to another day.

When I resumed my schedule in September, I realized how vital this time off had been. I had found a way to rest while still moving and in the process had rediscovered not only myself but also the heart and spirit of my work.

Stories for Along the Way: Jo on the Coast

A few years ago, on a cool California November day, I spent the most special day of my life just being with myself. My youngest son had left for college, and I found myself wondering who I was and what my purpose was. My primary job had been to be a mother for twenty-one years, yet it shocked me that I didn't have a clue what to do with myself.

I planned a day away from my crazy giving-to-everyone life. I headed toward the ocean with no clear destination in mind. Along the drive I stopped when I felt like it, taking photographs of vine-yards, eucalyptus trees, winding roads. I played my favorite music and pulled over to journal. Eventually I arrived at Bodega Bay, on a solitary beach. I noticed that I was one of only three people on the beach, and I was thrilled and a little unsure about being a woman all alone.

As I sat on the beach watching the waves, I completely lost track of time. I realized that this was the first moment of my entire adult life in which I didn't have somewhere to go, something to do, or someone to care for. It was just me, sitting on that warm, windy beach, alone. I felt so free and relaxed I got up and danced. I danced as if I were a little girl, twirling around and around. I buried myself in sand, feeling the earth support and nurture me. I have no idea how long I stayed, the waves dancing before me and me dancing with the waves. It was the experience of just "being" that brought me to my calm, true self.

Let go of

If I were suddenly infused with twenty times more courage, what would I let myself know? What depth of desire might reveal itself?

This is a good question to keep your hand moving till you fill up two pages, till you get past your internal censor. Or you might know the answer right off the top of your head!

How might allowing myself to remember that I am Divine, part of All That Is, help me rest this week, even in the midst of my busyness?

What role are shadow comforts and time monsters playing in my life these days?

How often do they substitute for genuine rest?

sunday   *monday*   *tuesday*

dates

_____

> *Meaning arises from loving life,*
> *not from goals or narrative.*
>
> — **Julio Olalla,** *The Ritual Side of Coaching*

Have to

What might change for me today if I found something to laugh at, or at least smile at, often?

Lightness encourages a change of mind, allowing you to drop the story that you don't have time to rest.

How can I love myself with food this week?

Make eating choices from a place of love instead of forcing yourself to be thin or "healthy."

Could do

I'm tolerating:

wednesday   *thursday*   *friday*   *saturday*

Intention:

Let go of

How much of my heart am I willing to shine out into the world?
Notice any negative thoughts you might have about being yourself or not being enough and shine anyway.

What am I most afraid of or worried about these days?
Name your fears. It helps.

What would help me soften toward one fear or worry right now?
When you find yourself making a choice that feels restricted, fearful, or heavy, breathe into wherever you feel the fear: stomach, neck, back, or solar plexus. Allow yourself to exhale some of your fear.

sunday	*monday*	*tuesday*

dates

Sew yourself a string of prayer flags to flap invitations to patience, clarity, and authentic trust into the heavens.

Have to

What love and attention would I like to give to my financial life this week?
Notice I said love, not guilt; this requires just one small act of attention, not a whole big plan.

What pleasure could color bring to me?
Some answers might be: buying a red cape or purple boots, sketching with colored pencils, digging through your closet for colors you haven't worn recently…

Could do

I praise myself for:

wednesday   *thursday*   *friday*   *saturday*

Intention:

Let go of

Where am I in respect to this moment? Where am I in respect to me?
Ask these questions throughout the week. Notice what you are drawn to, and name your next doable step toward sampling what beckons to you.

What do I choose to take responsibility for today? Perhaps something I've been blaming someone else for or avoiding noticing my part in?
No shame, and this doesn't have to be big. In fact, look for some small annoyance in your daily life and ask yourself how taking responsibility might offer you new possibilities.

sunday   *monday*   *tuesday*

dates

> *Delight has its own reward,*
> *adventure its own pleasure.*
>
> — **Kay Redfield Jamison,** *Exuberance*

Have to

I can tempt more breathing space and stillness into my life by...
Asking, "What can I let go of?" "Who can I ask for help?" and "Is this thought true?" can help.

What would it feel like to nurture someone I love this week by _____?
Conjure up what you would do and how it would feel. Notice any feelings of resentment or duty as well as of joy and lightness. Go toward the joy and lightness.

Could do

I'm grateful for:

wednesday   thursday   friday   saturday

Let go of

Source, I am ready to receive inspiration and guidance. What do I need to know?

As I consider the next few days, where do I automatically assume I don't have a choice in how I react, in what I do, say, and think? Where do I automatically defer or shape myself to someone else's plan or needs?

Write quickly, without editing; listen to your inner dialogue about choice.

What would I like to change about my plans for the next few days now that I see the new choices that are open to me?

sunday monday tuesday

dates

_____

It's hard to create something new until you are willing to be with what is.

Have to

What sensual beauty calls to me?
Lighting candles, cuddling a baby or kitten or puppy, buying an essential oil blend, savoring a ripe piece of fruit…

What relationship needs my attention this week — that with a partner, a friend I haven't spoken to in forever, a co-worker, a child, a pet, Spirit, nature?
Do you want to give that relationship attention?

Could do

I love:

wednesday   thursday   friday   saturday

21–24

The chambered nautilus offers
to you her secrets
wishes for the rhythm of the tides
to surge through your body.
So natural, this expanding, this contracting.

The honey-drunk honeybee offers to you
his exalted sweetness,
wishes for sipping the pollen of your life,
receiving each glistening drop.
So natural, this exuberance, this warmth.

The goose offers to you
her wild cry,
wishes that you too fly south to shelter
and rest in a still pond.
So natural, this migration, this leaving,
this returning.

Isn't it natural that the whole world wishes you well?

Stories for Along the Way: Amarja's Gratitude

When I had been trying to get pregnant for years and the baby that was floating around us and loved by us just didn't come into my arms, gratitude saved my sanity. I noticed I got more bitter and afraid as time went by; the fights with my partner became horrendous, and my heart was in such pain. I was getting really tired of focusing on what wasn't there, the lack, the missing baby in my arms. Since I didn't want to become old and bitter before my time, every night I wrote down — well, at least every other night — three things I felt gratitude for that day. It could have been what I ate that day, who I met, the cat's antics, the sun coming out, that I live in Amsterdam, that the computer worked. Sometimes I did things so I could later record them; thus gratitude began to infuse my actions. I became more and more aware of the blessings in my life. When I met a good friend after half a year of doing this practice and he asked me how I was, I said, "I am so blessed!" and that was a miracle.

Since then I have found my peace about not getting pregnant, and my motto has become "I want to do with you what spring does with the cherry trees," a verse from a poem by Pablo Neruda. What has been so important for me to learn is that the form you want something to take may not be the form that works, but the essence can come to you in so many ways.... Discerning the difference between form and essence has been the key for me, through focusing on what is present instead of what isn't.

Intention:

Let go of

What makes me sing with joy and jump out of bed at 6 a.m.? What do I have to pull myself away from?
If nothing does, what do you wish did? What attention will your joy receive this week?

If I were pushing or forcing or getting ahead of what is unfolding naturally, it would probably be in the area of _____.

Are my shadow comforts and time monsters making it easy to forget I am loved and supported by Spirit?

sunday   monday   tuesday

dates

_____

> *There is nothing besides the presence of God. Being itself is derived from God, and the presence of the creator remains in each created thing.*
>
> — Rabbi Menachem Nahum

Have to

Who am I being that allows others to shine?

This is a tongue twister of a question; allow it to twist open your mind. An example: I contain my energy and hold my tongue in certain situations so that my daughter can shine.

One basic need I'll nurture this week is:

Could do

I trust:

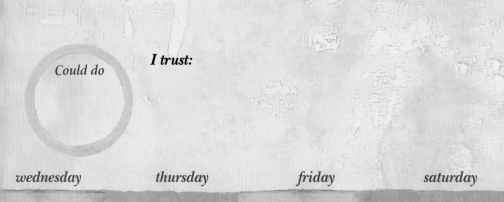

wednesday   thursday   friday   saturday

Let go of

What would truly nourish me today?

How often do we settle for a cookie or a TV show when what we really want is something much deeper?

Are my beliefs and private thoughts supporting me?

Listen in on what you are saying to yourself these days. Record the conversations right here, right now. Then take each thought and look for the facts — no adjectives or adverbs but provable, simple facts.

What one thought could I drop today?

Take one of your worries or negative thoughts and let it go.

sunday   *monday*   *tuesday*

dates

Your contentment and happiness are dependent
not on the events of your life
but rather on how you perceive those events
and choose to respond to them.

Have to

What does my heart need this week?
Check in and ask your heart.

What expression could my creativity exult in this week?
Maybe it's in writing a song, cooking a nourishing soup, creating
a scrapbook...

Could do

I giggle at:

wednesday   thursday   friday   saturday

Intention:

Let go of

What might help me live from the inside out in the next week?

Some answers could be: slowing down when you are driving, canceling one meeting, having lunch outside...

How can I support myself in making choices from my heart?

For me, it's spending time with people who love and trust me and who try to live from their hearts. Also, things like reading poetry by Hafiz and Rumi, biographies about people who lived their truth, and taking time in nature.

sunday   *monday*   *tuesday*

dates

Fill yourself a brimming cup of what
you truly desire, with a chaser of patience.
Say no to all else until the next step is revealed.

Have to

How could sound offer me sustenance this week?
Maybe you feel like listening to enlivening music, singing,
chanting, or toning.

Body, are you sending me any whispers, intuitions, or twinges that
I'm ignoring? If so, what message are you trying to give me?

Could do

I'm tolerating:

wednesday   *thursday*   *friday*   *saturday*

Intention:

Let go of

What do my actions and choices over the past three months or so reveal about what's most important to me?
Glance back over your Life Planner and your calendar; notice what you've spent your time and energy thinking about.

What and whom have I trusted in the past three months or so? How has faith in my deepest experiences made my life brighter or easier?
You may not realize the ways in which you are trusting or developing faith until you reflect.

When I look back over my "Have to," "Could do," "Let go of" lists for the past months and compare them to the lists of the months before that, what shifts do I see? What feels different?

sunday   *monday*   *tuesday*

dates

You are filled with multihued possibilities: glowing, lucid, verve filled, and dazzling.

Have to

What one shadow comfort or time monster am I ready to accept as part of me, for right now? What one thing am I ready to stop making excuses for, to stop feeling guilty about, and to gently embrace?

It might be eating chocolate, smoking on Friday nights, gossiping, going into debt from shopping, not filing your papers, avoiding checking your messages, pretending you're not doing something that you are doing, or saying that you'll stop doing it soon. Notice what is.

How has remembering my life insights changed the choices I've made or the reactions I've had?

Perhaps you sidestepped a boondoggle that might have consumed you previously or been able to stop a reaction that you don't find helpful.

Could do

I'm grateful for:

wednesday   thursday   friday   saturday

Whenever life makes itself known to you,
there is your path.
Whenever desire gives her come-hither look,
whenever trust flutters its wings,
whenever mystery is received into your belly,
there is your path.

Whenever time turns into prayer,
whenever love jiggles the doorknob,
whenever you rest in compassion,
There is your path.

Stories for Along the Way:
Melissa D.'s Deep Breath

I remember the moment. I wasn't on a yoga retreat, or
writing in my journal as I watched the waves roll in. I
was in my small New York apartment in Times Square
on the navy blue futon my boyfriend and I had recently

purchased. At twenty-six, I considered myself to be a somewhat enlightened young woman. Catching my breath from a run in Central Park, I grabbed the phone, eager to talk with my friend Lil, who had been trying to connect with me for several weeks. I shared about my unbelievable life — how madly in love I was with my wonderful boyfriend, how I loved the energy of living in this *amazing* city, how excited I was about my *fantastic* promotion, how *inspired* I was about this new aerobics class I was taking… what a *wonderful, amazing, exciting, fantastic, unbelievably inspiring* life it was.

Lil said, "You make me feel so tired — you're such a perfectionist with everything." This was not the reaction I was supposed to be getting. She was supposed to admire me, be envious of my wonderful life in New York, be inspired and acknowledge me for everything I've accomplished. I felt my heart grow heavy. Tears came to my eyes. I realized that I was performing in a play that I didn't write. I was doing all the things I thought made up a perfect, fulfilling, and wonderful life, yet I didn't feel fulfilled or happy. Slowly, I began to tell Lil how tired I was by the city's energy and how I could barely keep up with the pace; how my face had swelled up like the elephant man's the week before and how I spent most of the past week in a bathtub soaking in hot water to alleviate the shooting pains I felt throughout my body; how the doctor diagnosed my symptoms as borderline chronic fatigue syndrome (from working eighty-hour weeks?); how I couldn't stand aerobics and always looked longingly at the yogis breathing deeply into their chakras as I listened to my instructor tell me to lift my knees higher; how my job took everything out of me and I had little left for myself, my boyfriend, or my creative life; how I yearned to connect with her and other women. Lil and I took a deep breath together. For the first time in a long time, I looked outside and saw the glowing sun against the light blue sky. I saw children laughing as they played with the leaves in the fountain outside my window. That insight launched the journey back to myself.

I remember this insight and myself when I ring my meditation bells, light a candle, and meditate in the morning *before* checking my email and reading the *Wall Street Journal*. I remember myself when I make and bring chicken salad to work, even though the all-day meeting "includes lunch." I remember myself when I stand in tree pose in my yoga class, breathing deeply into my heart instead of exercising on level 11 on the elliptical. I remember myself when my colleague with two children asks me when I'm going to have children and I tell her that my husband and I have chosen, for now, not to. I remember myself when I can tell my friends and family that I had a tough week, and I'm scared about what's next instead of giving them a monologue of how wonderful my life is. I remember myself when I can ask other harried women trying to do it all, "When will it ever be enough?" and they begin to take a deep breath just like I did on that sunny fall day in New York City.

Stories for Along the Way: Melissa H. Walks

"It is solved by walking."

— Latin proverb

When I turned sixteen, I chose not to get my driver's license. A decade later that choice has resulted in the greatest spiritual gift I have. I walk everywhere. In walking, I find freedom and creativity.

Sometimes, I find peace. I am a worrier and a thinker. I live in a world of "what if" and "maybe." I live in my head — except when I walk.

Moving into my body usually takes me a couple of blocks of quick, long strides. I am not walking away from my head; I'm walking through the disconnect between head and body. Once I am in my body, I slow my pace because I no longer feel the need to push myself. That's when I start learning, connecting, and creating.

Walking allows my body to offer answers my mind doesn't have. I find solutions to tangles in my writing. I leave work behind and find ways out of my anxiety. Walking connects me to place. I walk to be healthy. I walk to be connected. I walk to be calm. I walk because I have to.

Intention:

Let go of

What or whom have I been envious of lately?

The power or creativity or boundaries that you see in others also live in you. What is one step you can take to develop what already lies within you?

What could I set right, forgive, or finish, that would allow me to connect with my love of life today?

Notice complaints, worries, feeling of heaviness or dread, or simply of bother. Focus on one concrete action.

sunday	*monday*	*tuesday*

dates

Spirit is delighted to dance with and through you, especially in the shadows and neglected places you believe are too ugly for love.

Have to

How have I started and ended my days in the past month? Does this help me set the tone for my day in a way I like, and do I have time to rest, reflect, or nurture myself at the end of some days?

What happens when I want something but I can't have it?
Do you often deny what you want? Do you ever challenge the idea you can't have _____? Do you give it to yourself anyway and then feel guilty?

Could do

I celebrate:

wednesday   thursday   friday   saturday

Intention:

Let go of

What part of my life, body, or emotions wants my attention? What do I wish to cherish and pay attention to?

Pause and listen, and then manage any feelings of being overwhelmed simply by choosing one item to focus on.

What request do I need to make, and of whom do I need to make it?

Write down any request you want to make. Be sure to state what you want, what result will satisfy you, and your deadline. "I want you to finish the taxes by Friday at the end of the day. I will be satisfied if you have itemized deductions in a Quicken report, with all the 1099s clipped together, and the phone bills itemized by business and personal calls." If you don't make clear requests, you can't create a life that fits you.

sunday   *monday*   *tuesday*

dates

"I accept" is your mantra.

Today, I am going to make my eating choices from a place of "How can I cherish myself more?" and that may mean that I . . .
Make one choice at a time: no big picture here, please.

How are my thoughts and private conversations supporting what I want to create in the world?
Listen in on what you are saying to yourself about what you want —
how possible or impossible it is, how worthy or unworthy you are.

I'm ready to let go of:

wednesday   *thursday*   *friday*   *saturday*

Let go of

How do I want to feel this week?

Remembering you have a choice is so delightful.

What does my body need to create the life I desire?

Energetically, physically, structurally — we can only have the life our body can support. Ask your body — not your mind — what it needs to support you. Fresh air, relaxed shoulders and open chest, awareness of your feet and grounding to the world, wide-open eyes, changing how you breathe — let your body help you.

| sunday | monday | tuesday |

dates

Decipher the Rosetta stone of creating your life:
you are enough, exactly the way you are.

Have to

How might I choose to have an impact on my world this week?
Perhaps you will inspire your world through your smile or your lasagna or your great idea about raising chickens. Note: *Your* world, not *the* world; what you *choose* to do, not what you *should* do.

What would help me love and accept the things I have to do this week?
We can get so particular about what we want to do that we slip into resentment about what we have to do (earn a living, wipe bottoms, cook dinner). What if instead you (attempt to) view these have-tos with gratitude?

Could do

I savor:

wednesday   *thursday*   *friday*   *saturday*

Intention:

Let go of

What is life calling forth from me this week? Do my four to six life focuses fit with where my passion wants to flow?

What minimum requirement of mine could use a little loving attention? Have I been forgetting something I need to be myself?

What life insight could make my life easier?

sunday   *monday*   *tuesday*

dates

_____

I won't bully myself to do better; I will love myself into discerning what my next step is.

Have to

What olfactory delights might nurture me?
Perhaps they are essential oils, grapefruit soap, ginger-almond lotion, Johnson's baby powder...

If I choose to share joy with another person this week, I might . . .
Of course, to share joy it helps to feel joy and to enjoy what you are offering. To give is to receive.

Could do

I believe:

wednesday   thursday   friday   saturday

29–32

A smorgasbord of silences:
Saturday-morning-before-anyone-but-you-is-awake
    silence.
The silence between you and your best friend when
    you say something important and you know
    she totally understands.
High-mountain silence.
The silence of a meditation that has smoothed you to
    weightless peace.
Under-warm-water silence.
The silence before you were born.

Stories for Along the Way: Karen's Retreat

Five years ago, I decided to treat myself to a week off
alone, to take a class, read, write, and reflect: a personal
retreat. I went to the library, looked up "retreats," and
found *The Women's Retreat Book*, which seemed to be
written just for me. I studied it carefully in planning
my time away, sticking little Post-its on all the pages I

wanted to use. I filled the trunk of my car with goodies: books of inspiration by women, soothing music, candles, art supplies.

On the third day of my retreat, I made a startling discovery: I had so much time to do whatever I pleased — reading, writing, walking, even napping. How was it that I never seemed to have any time at home for myself? Granted, I was exempt from laundry and meal preparation here, but how much time did those things really take? Wasn't every day made up of the same twenty-four hours? Even if I added housekeeping chores to a full workday and allowed eight hours for sleep, I should still have several hours left over. Where did that time go? I realized how much time I waste watching TV, playing on the computer, skimming the newspaper. I vowed to get some of those hours back and to build a tiny bit of retreat into every day.

Stories for Along the Way: Erin Listens

I always see the same image when someone asks me how I came to change my life: me as Wile E. Coyote, walking off a cliff into thin air, until I realize what I have done. I look down, but I don't fall. I keep walking off the edge of a cliff and into the beyond.

Two years ago, I walked off a cliff. I found myself traversing air and learning that the universe, it would seem, comes equipped with a safety net and a jet-propulsion system worthy of any Road Runner cartoon. All I have to add is the commitment to follow my heart.

For years, I was a workaholic corporate VP. I accepted every re-location and every promotion other people dreamed up for me, ig-noring the insistent little voice that kept asking, "But are you sure this is what you want?" I thrived on the travel, the frenetic pace, and the never-ending opportunities to save the day. I enjoyed the worship of eager young sales bucks. I liked never worrying about money. In a lot of ways, it was an easy life.

Only it wasn't mine.

I opened the door to change slowly. I tried to add balance by taking Spanish classes after work. Work got in the way. I booked thrilling vacations with friends, then canceled them for work. I signed up to mentor a young girl in Los Angeles and found myself pining for the riches of her Guatemalan family: community, creativity, the joys and pains of shared lives. The rewards of putting people first. Faith.

The little voice grew louder. When work grew more intense and more demanding, the voice told me to choose. I listened. I quit my job. I wanted to spend more time with this mysterious voice that I now recognized as my own. I longed to find the little girl who once came alive writing stories and playing music. I wanted to align my life with the voice, align my everyday actions with my heart and soul and values. I longed to feel at home in my life.

I put the voice in charge. I followed her to Spain, where a month-long Spanish course turned into two months and a reconnection with my childhood passion for languages and words. I followed the voice back to my beloved Chicago, selling my house in Southern California. I peeled off layers — habits, behaviors, and values — that no longer fit me. Continuing to trust my little voice, I turned down job after job, supporting myself with consulting projects, studying Spanish (because the voice loved it so), and traveling.

The voice began to ask — quietly — what I might learn about myself by living in Spain, speaking a new language and surrounded by another culture. How could I? How could I throw away the résumé I'd worked so hard to build? The voice wouldn't let me accept another "job," while the rest of me, afraid for my future, just kept applying for corporate jobs anyway. I was stuck.

Then one day, someone had the nerve to ask me what I would do if I could do anything, if nothing mattered, not money, not security, nothing. I finally let the voice answer: "I'd live in Spain. I am going to create a life in Spain." As soon as the words were out, the opportunities started showing up. I had learned the difference between saying no to what isn't authentically me, and saying yes to what is. Six months later I was living in Salamanca, Spain, immersed in the language I'd fallen in love with, living not five hundred meters from the Roman bridge I'd showed friends pictures of on the Internet when living here was only a dream.

Listening to the voice takes quiet and courage. The voice has led me back to music, to writing, to poetry. To the many and creative voices that make up the unique chorus I call Erin. Facing life choices, like my recent decision to work on my own, I now follow a simple rule. The heart — the voice — decides. Each member of the chorus will inevitably lobby her, and well they should, but in the end, the heart decides. We all agree that her choices bring the best return.

Let go of

What is beautiful, satisfying, filled with love, and blessed with grace about my life right now?
Oh, how wondrous to make this list!

When I consider the next few days, where do I automatically assume I can't — can't love myself, can't get something done, can't find the time, can't accept something?
Write quickly, without editing.... Listen to your inner dialogue concerning can't.

How, if at all, are shadow comforts and time monsters making noise in my life?
If they are, maybe it's okay with you right now. During times of stress or when you are working on one part of your life, it's okay to let other areas slide — it can actually be a good idea, as long as you are not sliding into addiction or ill health.

sunday   *monday*   *tuesday*

dates

Stop looking at the closed door, the lost opportunity, the if-onlys. Instead, breathe into the open passage that always leads to infinity — and beyond!

Have to

What one thing might I do this week, it if feels right, to make someone's life easier?

Think small. Look around your home, work, neighborhood. Get curious about how fun you can make it for yourself.

What physical organization does my life need this week?

Filing financial records? Sorting yarn or paint by color? Tearing out pictures and recipes and recycling the magazines afterward? Whatever you do, be sure it is small and you can finish!

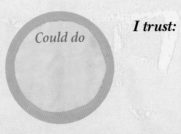

Could do

I trust:

wednesday   thursday   friday   saturday

Intention:

Let go of

How can I support myself in becoming the person I most want to be?

Asking this question usually involves stretching out of your comfort zone, taking a risk, and trying out something new.

What part of me needs attention this week?

Who wants your attention? Your six-year-old? Your creative self? Your rebel? Your critic? Ask this part of you what she needs to feel taken care of. You don't have to give her what she needs, but it is so comforting and healing just to listen to her.

sunday   *monday*   *tuesday*

dates

Expand your choices past what seems possible or reasonable, connect to what you truly want, and then see what is possible: a much bigger playing field!

Have to

What have I been giving to someone or something that I no longer want to give?

Helen, who attended a retreat, found that she no longer wanted to give her time to her twenty-two-year habit of watching a soap opera.

What do my surroundings reveal about me?

What does your desk say about you? Your bedroom? Your reading table? Your bathroom? Do you like what it reveals? What one change would make your daily life easier?

Could do

I'm ready to celebrate:

wednesday   *thursday*   *friday*   *saturday*

Intention:

Let go of

What do I want to accomplish this week?

Maybe it's a B+ on a paper, a clean desk, a date with your partner, an afternoon in nature.... Where is your energy naturally being drawn?

What thoughts might support me in enjoying my week?

Let these be truth-based, compassionate thoughts, especially about any stresses or challenges you may be facing.

What love can I share this week?

By sharing this love, you enlarge your own heart.

sunday *monday* *tuesday*

dates

> *Sacrifice is not giving up something to get something else you want more. Sacrifice is the art of drawing energy from one level and reinvesting it at another level to produce a higher form of consciousness.*
>
> — **Robert Johnson,** *Contentment*

Have to

What is the next doable step I could take this week to bring me into greater alignment with my financial well-being?

Take one step to improve whatever situation you're concerned about.

What is feeling less than clear or vibrant in my body? Are there any aches or twinges? Is there any dull or chronic pain I'd like to listen to and take care of?

Or maybe you'd like to keep ignoring them. It is in the choice that we find our truth.

Could do

I surrender to:

wednesday   thursday   friday   saturday

Intention:

Let go of

What do I need most this week?
Feel free to make a long list, and then choose one quality or action you can take that is not dependent on anyone else's actions or desires. "I need my boss/partner/child to be kind to me" can become "I find ways to choose peace around my boss/partner/child."

How active are the shoulds in my life these days?
Every time you hear a should, a have-to, or a must, ask yourself, "What do I want?"

What desire of mine could I share with someone I love?
Attend a class together, invite him or her into your studio to see what you just made, read a passage of a how-to book aloud...

sunday	monday	tuesday

dates

One definition of being spiritual is choosing to do only those things that contribute healing and meaning to one's life.

Have to

What would my creative self like this week?
Would it like new paints, time in nature, reading poetry until midnight (okay, maybe 10:30), guitar lessons…?

Where am I telling myself I must be different (smarter, kinder, faster, more organized) than I currently am? In what area of my life am I critical of how I'm showing up?
What might change if you accepted how you are in this situation, if you really let it be okay? I'm not saying make yourself accept it, but imagine what might change if you could.

Could do

I'm ready to receive:

wednesday   thursday   friday   saturday

33–36

When anything turns into a should (also known as something we *have* to do, because we think it's the right way, the way it's done), we lose touch with the present moment. Feeling, choice, and the ability to discern what is best for us drain out of whatever activity or relationship has become a should.

Me and the shoulds, we go way back. I first noticed how thoroughly they had invaded my life when I realized the first thought in my head every morning was "I should get up." Before my feet even hit the floor, *the choice about how to shape my day was not my own*. Deanna describes her experience with shoulds as the "should shovel," as in, "I should do my insurance paperwork; however, I really want to take a nap, but I won't allow myself the pleasure of a nap, so I go eat. The should shovels food into my mouth. I don't do what I really want, so I eat."

Shoulds eat up life, deny us personal choice, and allow us to hide behind what is "right" without ever considering what we want until we gently transform them with the light of compassionate awareness. It can feel easier to hide behind a should instead of coming into the present, feeling your desire, and choosing. If you say, "I should work all weekend" instead of "I choose to spend my time working instead of with my family," you don't really have to take responsibility for the life you're creating. It is vaguely "over there" with your boss or your need to make the mortgage payment.

Stories for Along the Way: Monica's Story

I was lying on the floor with a crushing pain in my chest, struggling to inhale. I was sure I was having a heart attack, and that I probably deserved it, because bad things only happen to bad people, right? This was a very bad thing, so I must be very bad. The pain in my chest was so intense that I, who never asked for help and did everything by myself, actually called out to God, in frantic, terrified prayer. The pain did not stop. I was petrified, certain I was going to die, and that I would die without ever having done any of the things I'd always wanted to do, without seeing the things I'd always wanted to see.

I tried bargaining: pleading and promising that I'd be good, I'd be so good from now on if this "punishment" would stop. I started to be calm, believing if I were truly good, I would be helped. The pain diminished, faded, finally left. I knew it was because I had made the promise to be good. And something bothered me about that.

I wondered what kind of God would send a sudden, violent sickness to me for the purpose of letting me know I'm bad, to threaten me with even worse punishments if I didn't submit to being good. I realized I did not truly believe that God, if there was a God, would be so dominating and cruel. Then I wondered (now on my way to the doctor's office) what was going on with me that I should have this life-changing event, this brush with mortality, the fear that I deserved pain and punishment. A thought rose up from deep inside me, a new voice so sincere, so accurate, so true: the knowledge, that I was —

Not so bad.

Not as bad as I had always feared I truly was. Not so bad as to deserve such a fright, to deserve such crushing pain, to spend each day with no time to rest, no time to play, no time to just be.

Later, when I called my boss and told her how sick I had been all night and that I was waiting for test results and needed a couple of days off, she said, "Is your work caught up?" I wondered why she did not even ask about my being sick. I thought I was caught up on my work, so I took two days off. I went back to work, even though I wasn't feeling well, but I was afraid of all the work that was piling up and believed I had to be there, no matter what. When I got in that morning, there was an angry voice mail from my boss: "Your report is a week late!" I thought about that.

I thought about the past year on this job, and all the overtime I had routinely put in, all the times I had come in sick, meeting the demands to do three and four jobs besides my own. I thought about how, even though my boss said the quality of my work was "exceptional," I thought I was bad because sometimes some of my paperwork was late, and that "good" meant doing much too much work, much too fast, and for too many hours to be healthy.

I thought about God.

I thought about being not so bad.

I realized my boss was not God. And I realized the voice I'd listened to all my life, the one that said I had to do everything for everybody else, that my needs did not matter, no matter how well I performed, or what my talents were, that I had to ignore those talents because following my own path was selfish — I realized that that voice was not God, either. Then it occurred to me that being good might have something to do with hearing my own voice and following where it leads. I started looking for another job. More important, I started listening carefully to this inner voice, to learn where my real talents lie and what I want to give to this life.

I think, I really, honestly think, that's...not so bad.

Stories for Along the Way: Angel's Gentle Nudges

I've stopped trying to force myself to do something I think I "should" do at any given moment. What I do now is pause for a moment to allow my intuition to tell me what needs to be done next. It feels like a quiet nudging sensation in my gut. When I follow this gentle nudging, I feel very calm and purposeful about what I am doing. It doesn't matter what it is — folding laundry, sweeping the front porch, invoicing clients, designing a logo, walking the dog. My energy flows freely, and it feels like I have more time, perhaps because my heightened presence allows me to use my time efficiently, mindfully, without thoughts of what else I "should" be doing. The more I allow this nudging sensation to guide my activity, the more amazed I am at how nothing seems to fall between the cracks — I don't forget things, and I don't commit to things I don't want to do. I have come to trust this process completely.

Intention:

Let go of

As I see my life as an act of devotion to Spirit, what am I drawn to do, create, or be?
Allow this question to tickle you; take it into meditation or on a walk, or sketch a response.

What projects, relationships, or boondoggles, if any, are currently weighing on me?
Take a moment to name whatever is bugging you, and be with it for a few moments, breathing and accepting what is.

What is the next doable step I need to take in one of these situations or projects?
Choose only one situation and take one step.

sunday   monday   tuesday

dates

_____

Surrender your shoulds; discover your desires.

Have to

How could a nap or a mini-retreat help me be true to myself this week?
If you quip, "You've got to be kidding — me, rest?" that is the clearest sign you need to, and soon!

What creative treat or spiritual connection could replace an outmoded shadow comfort or time monster or simply something I'm bored with?

Could do

I am deserving of:

wednesday   thursday   friday   saturday

Let go of

What brings me joy? How do I want that joy to express itself in my life today? This week?

Joy in the moment reconnects us with life, with purpose and flow, and it dissolves stubborn have-tos.

What or who is giving me energy these days?

List everyone and everything that is energizing you, and take a moment to be grateful.

What quality would I like to call in from the Divine or nature this week?

It might help to look at what is looming over you or stressing you, and ask what you might need to help you.

sunday   *monday*   *tuesday*

dates

_____

Praise precedes faith.

— **Abraham Heschel**

Have to

What could I choose to do that might help to heal someone in my community?
The person in need of help may not get what you are offering. Your job is to be inspired and to put it out there — that's all.

What shall I do for fun, silliness, laughing until I pee my pants this week?
Please don't skip this question because you are too busy — that is when you most need fun!

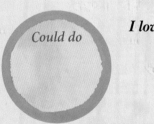

Could do

I love:

wednesday   thursday   friday   saturday

Let go of

What is the relationship between health and self-love for me right now?
When I hate myself, I hurt myself with food. What about you?

What small act of self-kindness could help me love myself more in my relationship to money?
Maybe it's packing your lunch this week, actually opening and reading your retirement account statements, researching how to increase your prices or how to ask for a raise, networking with ten people, or congratulating yourself on some aspect of your finances.

sunday   *monday*   *tuesday*

dates

_____

Beyond here and there
Beyond words
Is the creative spark that holds you, and I,
in the palm of its hand.

Have to

What resources do I need to call on this week to take action on a dream?
What help might you be willing to ask for and receive?

What does it mean for me to be healthy?
Explore for a moment the question of health and what it means for you today.

Could do

I'm itching to:

wednesday   thursday   friday   saturday

Let go of

What have I been creating in the past three months?
Is it peace, love, support, intimacy...sketches, essays, poems, gardens...more money, better health, more pleasure...?

When I look back over my "Have to," "Could do," "Let go of" lists for the past three months and compare them to my to-do lists before that, what shifts do I notice?

As I look back, when have my shadow comforts been most active? What about my time monsters?
Name the times, the triggers, and what happened (or didn't happen).

sunday   *monday*   *tuesday*

dates

You are always surrounded by the support of your allies, hands of compassion and trust, of passion and praise, gently patting your back, urging you forward.

Have to

How has remembering my life insights helped me? Is it time to add new ones to the list or to rewrite any of the existing insights?

This process is all part of being a work in progress.

What direction is my life headed in these days? If I were a poet, how might I sum up where I'm going?

Indulge your imagination, and let it speak to you in metaphor. Let yourself be surprised.

Could do

I am honored to:

wednesday   thursday   friday   saturday

37–40

Camus advised, "Live to the point of tears."
I understood that once.
But then I forgot.
In the times of forgetting I wish for me
and for you
a universe of candlelight to echo the light within
a volcano of possibilities,
a basket of warm bread, big enough to feed all who
    are ravenous, within and without,
and the knowing that suffering can be a grace, the
    doorway to an awakened heart.

Stories for Along the Way: Shannon's Bowl

My process of growth and change is usually marked by a time of darkness followed by an emerging light. In the winter of 2004, everything was changing. My job of the past seven years was about to end. One of my closest friends, who happened to be my only single friend, had become engaged. I suddenly felt like I was losing everything.

When I am feeling off balance and unsure of what to do, I go either to my favorite waterfront or, if it's dark, to a pier near my house.

It was almost midnight when I walked to the end of the pier, carrying my sadness and fear and emptiness. I leaned on the railing and cried. Then I started to sing "Amazing Grace." Something about that song had always comforted me.

As I sang, a vision floated into my head. I was holding a purple pottery bowl. There was a hole in the bottom, and the contents of the bowl were slowly draining out. It was emptying itself. Exactly what was happening to me.

Soon, the bowl was empty, yet my heart began to fill. There was nothing in the bowl because it was a vessel waiting to be filled. A space full of the possibility of what would come next. I knew that I would be taken care of. I would not be alone. I might not know what was coming, but there would always be more to fill my bowl, if I was willing to wait, watch, and listen.

I took a deep breath and realized my hands were outstretched, as if I were actually holding the bowl. I had stopped singing at some point, and my heart was filled with the serenity I usually feel only when I'm listening to "Amazing Grace."

As I lowered my hands, I looked up. The clouds parted to reveal an almost full moon.

Intention:

Let go of

What small shift in my thinking might make this week easier and more delightful?

You might look back to your list of what you resent, or you might make a list of your current complaints or numb spots and see what true and nourishing thought could change your perception.

What personal limit am I denying or pushing against?

Perhaps it's how much sleep you need, how much time you spend alone, the kinds of food you thrive on but aren't giving yourself, the amount of nature, fresh air, or exercise you need…

What gift can I effortlessly reveal in the coming days?

Without effort, without straining, what can't you help but give? Are you letting it be enough? Letting it out into the world?

sunday   *monday*   *tuesday*

dates

_____

The most ravishing experience you can have
is of the mysterious, of living in consecrated curiosity,
with the symphony of the universe playing through you
and the still point laying claim to your heart.

Have to

What act of self-kindness would strengthen me this week?

Perhaps you could declare a blame and complaint fast. For a day or longer, every time you hear yourself, silently or aloud, blaming or complaining, stop.

What one small detail, if I addressed it, would make my daily life easier?

Never being able to find your keys (install a hook by the door); no place to recycle (place bins under the sink); no time to return phone calls (get a headset so you can do dishes, fold laundry, even exercise while talking); dark bathroom (buy a lighted magnifying mirror). Address one detail this week.

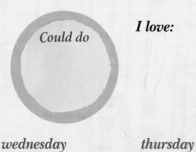

Could do

I love:

wednesday   *thursday*   *friday*   *saturday*

Let go of

What is one fear, anxiety, or uncomfortable place in my life right now? What is it stopping me from doing, feeling, or being?
You can name more than one, and then focus on just one.

If I were somebody who could achieve _____ [whatever the fear or anxiety is stopping you from doing], what would I be able to do?
Sometimes it helps to choose a role model — Joan of Arc, Coretta Scott King, your Aunt Louise — and imagine what she would do. Feel free to generate a big list of doable actions, and then choose one next step.

What media experiences have I been imbibing lately? What media experiences would it be nurturing to let go of?
We are shaped and influenced by what we watch, read, and listen to.

sunday   *monday*   *tuesday*

dates

_____

Fear is a contraction that melts when it is listened to and accepted.

Have to

What personal grooming habit am I ready to let go of?
We get into ruts about what we must do — color our hair, iron clothes, wear mascara. What are you ready to let go of — just for this week — for the sake of simplicity or creating time?

If there were something I needed to grieve, it might be . . .
Whether what you need to grieve is specific or nameless, old or timeless, personal or simply about the state of the world, when might you create some time and space to let your grief flow?

Could do

I've always wanted to:

wednesday   *thursday*   *friday*   *saturday*

Intention:

Let go of

What would help me go with the flow of life this week?

How can I nurture my body so that I am taking care of myself in sync with the season?
What are you doing for exercise, what you are eating, how much rest are you getting?

What is hanging on the edge of my consciousness that I'm ready to be aware of?
How does letting yourself know increase your trust and faith?
What one doable step can you take based on this knowledge?

sunday   *monday*   *tuesday*

dates

_____

Invite little pauses into your day, spiritual catnaps
that let your heart catch up with the rest of you.

Have to

What am I willing to celebrate about myself this week?
To notice and applaud?

When will I be in nature this week?
Where do you yearn to be? Lying on the earth, weeding your garden, sitting by the ocean?

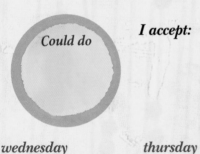

Could do

I accept:

wednesday   thursday   friday   saturday

Intention:

Let go of

How often am I meeting my minimum requirements?
Here's another way to say it: How firm is your foundation?
What cracks need attention? Choose only one thing, and
break the remedy down into doable steps.

**How do I like to nurture myself? What truly feeds and
replenishes me?**
Notice, too, the last time you gave yourself some of this feed-
ing and replenishing.

sunday   *monday*   *tuesday*

dates

_____

Self-nurturing is a caramelized topping over a trust brûlée: you've got to have the trust, or you are left with just burnt sugar: sweet but brittle and not very satisfying.

Have to

I've been forgetting a life insight lately, and the way I'd like to remember it is by _____.
Maybe you'd like to remember by creating a mixed-media collage, writing a poem or story about it, or sharing it with someone in conversation.

How do I choose to spend my time this week? Who do I choose to spend my time with? Again, think about your choices.
It is your choice!

Could do

I praise myself for:

wednesday   thursday   friday   saturday

41-44

Thomas Edison was old and he had a hunger
That had never been quenched,
him being nearly deaf most of his life.

So he hired a pianist to come and play great waltzes. Loud.
"Louder, play louder," he shouted.
The man played louder,
and then louder still.
Edison shook his head.

The inventor rolled his desire around on his tongue:
and then he lunged,
sunk his teeth into the piano leg, and
held on like a dog.

Schubert tuned his vertebrae,
Strauss tickled his mandible,
Chopin tootled and tingled every phalange.
Edison swallowed. Sat back on his heels and nodded
in time with the beat.

Essential Gadgets for the
Ordinary Divine Woman

Energy Depleter Detector Ring: Available in five fashion colors, the Energy Depleter is discreet yet insistent. A gentle buzz alerts you whenever anyone or anything is sucking you dry. Should you fail to protect yourself, the Energy Depleter Ring will give you a light electrical shock. Should you continue to remain obtuse, the electrical shock will increase until it is the equivalent of a cattle prod (similar to the prod you can use on partners, children, and co-workers when they refuse to do what you have politely asked them to do).

Guilt Be Gone Balm: Provides long-lasting shine.

Boundary Shrink Wrap: Available in extra large for the holidays.

Self-Doubt Stain Remover: Removes fresh and stubborn stains and discourages revisiting stale doubts and thoughts of would'a, could'a, should'a.

Discontent Force Field: Consumer culture getting you down? Meaningless distractions or tedious comparisons making it difficult for you to appreciate your own irreplaceable beauty and inspiring gifts? Caring too much about what others think? Press the on button and feel all that meaningless discontent evaporate! Warning: Real discontent may seem temporarily magnified. Manufacturer takes no responsibility for any life changes that may result.

Divine Hearing Aid: New and improved model amplifies guidance up to 1,000 percent, including the guidance you pretend not to hear; never needs batteries, powered by All That Is.

Oil of Optimism: Three drops will lighten your load.

Stories for Along the Way: Sally's Self-Care Revival

Married at twenty, a mother at twenty-four, all I'd pretty much done in my life was care for others. My self-care experiences were limited. I squeezed my master's degree and my doctorate in between breast-feeding, going to church, working, attending my daughter's Irish dance lessons, going to teacher conferences, doing housework, spending time with my husband. Take a break? Sure, someday. Sleep? A little, after the work was done. Exercise? Who has time? The result? I was seventy-five pounds overweight, suffering from high blood pressure, high cholesterol, and high blood sugar. I was a heart attack or a stroke waiting to happen. A pounding twenty-four-hour headache was my wake-up call. After I left the clinic, I took the advice of my physician and made my first massage therapy appointment. Thus began my journey toward self-care.

I began (guiltily) having twice-monthly massages. A few months later, a friend suggested I try Reiki. I began to come awake to my life, as if from a long sleep. I found the courage to quit my job at a non-profit and begin working full-time in my own business. People noticed I was happier and more relaxed. Then I realized my marriage was in trouble, but I felt helpless to do much. However, I knew it was critical for me to become healthy. The weight had to come off.

I found myself in a dance-fitness class called Nia. I took off my shoes and socks and stood in the back, thinking, "I can't possibly do this!" I was far too embarrassed even to consider wearing exercise clothes. My knees hurt. My feet hurt. I felt very out of place. Then the teacher called a friendly welcome to me and started the class. No one stared; they just smiled and went on dancing. None of them had perfect, size-6 bodies. Most were lumpy and bumpy just like me, and I saw many smiles and satisfied expressions.

I began to attend a Nia class each week. At first, I couldn't even make it through a full class, I was so unfit. A teacher patiently worked with me one-on-one, and I graduated to a full class, although I remained in the back of the room, avoiding the mirror's gaze and the teacher's attention. I grew more confident and joined a weight-loss program. I radically changed my diet. Slowly, I began to increase the number of Nia classes I attended, and I also began to attend yoga classes. Then I bought a bicycle — my first in a dozen years! After eighteen months I had lost nearly fifty pounds and had dropped four clothing sizes.

I no longer take any medications, and all my blood tests are normal. I chose to end my marriage because my partner had a destructive lifestyle, and I couldn't live that way anymore. I developed a yoga practice that sustained me through the difficult end of our relationship. I rode in a three-hundred-mile bike tour, something I never imagined I would do. I became a certified Nia teacher and now teach five classes a week. I'm learning to live from my center: I meditate each day; I read inspirational writers; I attend rituals and worship activities; I connect to what is universal and holy, and this nurtures me. I often get up at 5 a.m. to make sure I have self-care time before my workday.

I now stand at the front of the room during Nia class, looking right in the mirror, smiling and leading the dance, and loving the woman I see (even though I still need to lose twenty-five pounds). I've finally found ME — a writer and a dancer. I can give so much more to the world when I give to myself first.

Let go of

What would I choose to do this week if I remembered that I am a quirky, fabulous, utterly unique and perfect as I am?

My mood lately has been...
Take note of your most frequent background moods. Becoming aware of your mood allows you to decide if you want to intervene, and if so, how.

Is pushing, forcing, striving, or doing excessively for others present in my life these days? If so, is that okay with me?
No judgment, just awareness.

sunday   *monday*   *tuesday*

dates
_____

Construct a raft of compassionate self-care,
nourishing support, and constructive, well-grounded
thoughts to carry you where you wish to go.

Have to

What would nurture my soul this week?
Sit back, let out a sigh, and listen.

What self-nurturing could I share with someone I love?
Light a candle for someone, and spend a few moments sending him
or her acceptance, love, and compassion. Imagine this loved one
surrounded by a band of allies — living and dead, real and imagi-
nary — aiding and supporting, guiding and loving.

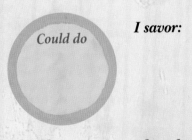

Could do

I savor:

wednesday   *thursday*   *friday*   *saturday*

Intention:

Let go of

What is beckoning to me these days?
Remember that the presence of an edge of fear or uncertainty does not mean that you should not answer the call; it only means that you must take one small step and then listen again.

What doable step could I take to explore this call?

To paraphrase Mary Oliver, what would help me love the soft animal of my body today?
What helps your flesh feel accepted and treasured?

sunday   *monday*   *tuesday*

dates

_____

Feel yourself beloved on this earth.

Have to

What shadow comforts or time monsters are no longer serving me?
You may notice habits that have dropped away naturally; if so, be sure to celebrate that shift. Or perhaps a shadow comfort or time monster is just not doing it for you anymore, not giving you what you need, and you are ready to ask, "What do I really want?"

Who could I see as holy today? Who could I greet as a part of the light within us all?
Let this answer unfold as your day does. Don't assume you already know.

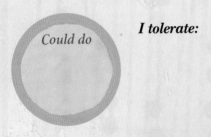

Could do

I tolerate:

wednesday   thursday   friday   saturday

Let go of

What area of my life or what role [as partner, business owner, artist, mother, caretaker, chauffeur] could benefit from loving acceptance and nourishing attention this week?

Notice where your attention is naturally drawn or what area of your life you feel uneasy about or disconnected from. Note one or two doable steps you can take. Brainstorm how different areas can support instead of stress each other.

Would one of my minimum requirements help me flow between areas of my life with more grace?

Look back at your list to see if you would benefit from more attention to your basics.

What secret grace might I offer the world this week?

Some possibilities: leaving a love note in the break room at work, leaving the garbagemen muffins, sending money anonymously to someone you know is a little short this month...

sunday   *monday*   *tuesday*

dates

_____

A thunderbolt illuminates your heart:
it isn't your job alone to fulfill your dreams
and give birth to your yearnings.
You can relax and ask for help,
and help will come.

Have to

Is there someone in my life with whom I'd like to be closer?

Is it a co-worker, your child, your mother...?

What one small change would I love to make in what or how I eat this week?

What beckons to you? A particular fruit or veggie? Eating mindfully? Fresh juice? A day of fasting? Experimenting with a new recipe?

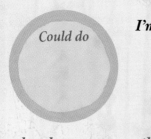

Could do

I'm ready to receive:

wednesday   *thursday*   *friday*   *saturday*

Let go of

What quality would I most like to share with, offer to, and beam out into the world today?

Is it lightness, generosity, gratitude, perspective, patience, laughter? Or…?

What fosters contentment in my life? What, if anything, nudges me toward discontent?

Perhaps you could make a two-column list, with things that foster contentment on one side and things that lead to discontent on the other. Study the list once or twice in the next week and see what occurs to you.

sunday   *monday*   *tuesday*

dates

May you always have the ears to hear, the determination to see, the courage to create.

Have to

What is bugging me, or pushing me, or making me feel off-kilter?

When was the last time I laughed at the absurdity of life?
Monty Python re-runs always help me.

Could do

I'm enjoying:

wednesday   thursday   friday   saturday

45–48

To live a life that is yours, you must be willing to be imperfect and humble, lost and fuzzy *often*. To be willing to declare you don't know. If fact, *I don't know* can become your favorite words.

You get more comfortable or at least more familiar with hanging out in the gap between what you want to create, experience, and feel and what actually is. Your ability to stay conscious and compassionate in this gap is what will propel you forward.

When you don't get to what you care about, be it greater intimacy with your partner, the plan for your business, your novel, your easel, or a kayaking trip down the Amazon, it's not because you are too busy — that excuse is almost always bullshit. You don't go there, or stay there long enough once you do go, because to be there, over and over again, is to be with, to live with, and to breathe into the realization that what you are creating doesn't express exactly what you yearn for.

To be alive is to be on your knees, humbled as you

fall in love with the perfection of imperfection, as you become familiar with loving the gap.

Stories for Along the Way: Andrea's Knowing

"Don't tell me about what you fear. Tell me about what you know."

My friend Jason said this to me when I first started my jewelry business. I was telling him how much I loved making jewelry, how I wanted my business to be successful, and how it didn't seem it would ever be profitable. I was in tears by the end of the conversation, telling him all the reasons why it wouldn't work.

Then he asked me that question: "Not your fear, Andrea, but what do you *know*?" He stopped me in my tracks.

I found myself saying, "I know I'm creating something special. I know it will work eventually. I know it will take some time and staying steady. I know I can stay with it through the hard parts. I know I don't want to quit."

I did stick with it. There were hard parts. There were more tears and more days of wanting to quit, but when I checked in, when I asked myself that one question, it was a key to my wiser self. My wiser self wanted me to keep going. She was right.

When I think of getting pregnant these days, when I get really, really afraid, and I'm moving through the darkest places, I stop myself and ask myself what I know. Because what I know is that I'm creating something special, that it's going to work eventually, that it will take time and steadiness, and that I can stay with it through the hard parts.

Somehow I know this is much closer to the truth than all my fear.

Let go of

What would I do differently this week if I was willing to hang out in the gap between what I want and where I am?

What would you do differently in the next ten minutes? The next hour? Tonight?

What self-nurturing activities might increase my courage to be in the gap?

You might try inhaling and saying, "I am life," and on your exhale saying, "Breathing." Or you might imagine calm, loving energy as a color filling up your heart. Allow the color to swirl around, charging you with peace and courage. Place your hand on your heart and repeat the word *love* to yourself.

What do I find myself complaining about lately? What do I say I don't have time or energy for?

Complaints point to self-nurturing opportunities.

sunday   *monday*   *tuesday*

dates

_____

Who publishes the sheet-music of the winds, or the
written music of water written in river-lines?

— John Muir

Have to

If I decided to choose one life insight to guide my
week, I would choose:

If I decided to forgive myself for something this week, I would
choose:

Could do

I tolerate:

wednesday   thursday   friday   saturday

Intention:

Let go of

What one area of my life do I wish to focus on and nurture this week?

Your health, one friendship, one parenting skill, one area of work...

If I planned my week with an attitude of play and ease, I would choose to . . .

Allow your playful self to dream aloud.

sunday   *monday*   *tuesday*

dates

_____

Love fashioned from breath, anchored to purpose,
and yet still unfettered, going where it is needed.

Have to

What am I mulling over these days?
Are these thoughts truthful? Are they supportive of the direction you are headed in?

If I opened my heart and connected with someone in my life this week, I would...
You can open your heart and connect, even if the other person doesn't respond the way you would like.

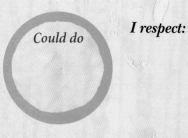

Could do

I respect:

wednesday   thursday   friday   saturday

Let go of

What wants to be at the heart of my life today?
What wants to be your focus? This question can lead you to your intention.

What choices could I make today to create an exquisite, magnificent, sparkling-with-life week?
If necessary, let your critic have its complaint fest about why this question is a silly waste of time. Then focus on the word *choose* as you go about your week.

sunday   *monday*   *tuesday*

dates

Let the light radiate from you and through you.
Surrender and allow your greatness to shine forth.

Have to

What, if anything, needs emotional healing in my soul right now? What needs gentle attention?
What part of you would like to be heard?

If I finished _____, it would be very self-nurturing.
Asking this question doesn't mean you have to finish it; just be willing to acknowledge the possible relief or the satisfying sigh that might follow completion.

Could do

I honor myself for:

wednesday   thursday   friday   saturday

Let go of

When I spend time with or work with _____, I feel enlivened. I'd like to deepen that relationship by...

What do I most want to embrace about myself or someone this week?

It may be something you can't fathom and keep rejecting as bad or annoying, such as your partner's snoring or your habit of gnawing your nails; it may be something that pops into your head right this moment.

The quality I'd like to invite into my life from the Divine is _____, and I will invite this quality in by _____.

sunday   monday   tuesday

dates

_____

*All we know, all we have, is this moment,
and the more we can open to and accept life
as it is unfolding right now, the more we will live
in the perfection of true peace.*

Have to

I want to play with:
Are you drawn to watercolor crayons, a computer program, a drawing technique, a mountain, a dog, a friend, a lover, a kite...?

One small step I am willing to take toward my financial well-being this week is:
Only commit to what you are actually able and willing to do.

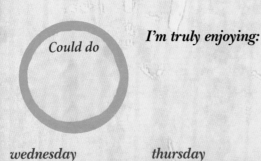

Could do

I'm truly enjoying:

wednesday   thursday   friday   saturday

49–52

I open my front door to get the morning paper, and the world stuns me. Warm tropical waters lap at my toes, ice drips off the twigs of a gnarled apple tree, and across the street, the rusty textured door of a cobalt blue home in Santa Fe glows. But wait, I don't live in Santa Fe.

A junkyard, a yard sale, the flea market to end all flea markets, an auction of mythical gardens and Joseph Cornell shadow boxes have appeared in my side yard. A miniature Alaskan Arctic Refuge bulges and arches in my driveway, and the Prado and the Louvre stand where, last night, my neighbor's roses budded.

I need to write in my journal and take pictures of all this, but there's no time; now people are spilling down my street with their stories and their eyes, eyes that improvise a river of compassion. Hours, days, eons pass as we look into each other's universes and smile, here and there, an unexpected wink at just the right time. We are fearless in our connections, inspired.

It is morning, after all, and so I begin to think about tea, jasmine tea, white tea, Yorkshire Gold tea with cream in my grandmother's teapot — then the books arrive — thousands and thousands. There are fun but flawed novels (the perfect ones sometimes make me never want to write again), biographies of Georgia O'Keeffe and Eleanor Roosevelt, philosophy, and spirituality. And the poetry! Mary Oliver, Theodore Roethke, Pablo Neruda, Rumi, Billy Collins, Walt Whitman... the blessing of words raining down.

Swooning with language, I dig my hands into the patch of garden closest to the door, to feel myself on this earth, and the surprising scent of mint arises. I inhale. A breeze drifts by, carrying the smells of cut grass, Durga Rose incense, nutmeg, the Indian spice shop in Berkeley, the Asian supermarket in the international district, the cedars on Bear Island.

Now the inspiration comes with the full force of love: images of New York skyscrapers, a great piece of theater, an early fall morning in the Appalachians, a bonfire on the beach in winter, someone's truth heard, synchronicity, silence in a circle of women, my body moving, the birth of babies and grandbabies and nieces and nephews, color, paint, images, beads.

I have to lie down. The porch feels cold through my robe. Quiet descends, the quiet of driving in the car without the radio on, of eating alone, of taking communion. The quiet morning murmurs that it is time to listen and get directions for the day, week, month ahead.

I'm gifted with a new day.

I go inside to finally make tea. I leave the door open. Who knows what might wander in?

Stories for Along the Way: Merri's Listening

Cancer doesn't run in my family. I didn't know much about it when my doctor told me the biopsy results revealed that I had diffused large B cell lymphoma. I didn't even know that he was telling me I had cancer until he said he was referring me to an oncologist. I *knew* what that meant. I received a gift that day, though I wouldn't realize it for many months, and it wouldn't feel like a gift on long chemo days and nights when I was wide awake at 3 a.m. feeling alone, small, and like the "me" I had always known was disappearing. Yet the me I had always known wasn't lost, but going through a metamorphosis. I was becoming stronger through my vulnerability, even as I was feeling weaker by the minute. With each passing chemo treatment (and the slew of side effects), my life slowed to a snail's pace, until time was suspended and I noticed a new leaf beginning to sprout on a plant, the feel of the blanket fibers on a prayer quilt, the comfort of a cool washcloth on my forehead.

I had done everything fast — talk, eat, work, play. After all, wasn't life supposed to be lived, and isn't time short? Perhaps my pace eventually would have led to burnout, high anxiety, possibly a heart attack, but Spirit had a different plan. One I wasn't aware of at the time — I sure wish I'd been let in on the secret!

On one of those chemo nights when I was wide awake, I asked, "Who am I if I can't be working, or if I can't physically help people anymore because I don't have the strength, or be there to drive family members to their doctor appointments? Who am I if all I can be is someone lying in a bed, feeling horrible, and having no energy?" The answer didn't come immediately, but when it did, it was gentle and soothing. I knew it was an answer from God. It was like light breaking across the mountains in the morning:

> You are a child of God.
> You are a trusted friend.
> You are an inspirer of dreams.
> You are an encourager.
> You know who you are, deep inside you
>   know.
> Don't allow this world to define who
>   you are.
> You are in this world, not of this world.

It was the first time I had valued myself for who I was at my core rather than for what I could do. To be a trusted friend, an inspirer of dreams or an encourager, I didn't need to be a computer genius, to lift heavy furniture, to walk for miles, to drive a car, or even to have energy. I only needed heart and soul — and I had always had plenty of that.

My favorite scripture verse is "The light shines in the darkness and the darkness cannot overcome it" (John 1:5).

Let go of

Where does my energy want to flow this week?
What is the easiest way for me to approach today?

What is falling through the cracks of my life these days?
Maybe nothing is. Or maybe it's something you can't quite put your finger on, so you might need to take time to breathe or check in with your body or with a trusted friend or adviser.

What have I allowed myself to receive lately?
Make a list. Looking at your calendar or emails might help jog your memory.

sunday   *monday*   *tuesday*

dates

_____

> ### *The work is remembering to play.*
>
> — **Deborah Hay**

Have to

How have I been talking to myself recently?
Are you speaking to yourself as you would someone you love and cherish?

If I had to think of a relationship that I'm ready to take some time away from or let go of, the one that would come to mind is _____.

Action is not necessary, if you aren't sure or ready. Simply to acknowledge that you might be ready to change a relationship — to a person, thing, habit, practice, place, technology, or comfort — can be helpful.

Could do

I praise:

wednesday   *thursday*   *friday*   *saturday*

Intention:

Let go of

How could I live this week as if I believed I was enough?
Notice what this idea feels like in your body. From the place of *enough*, what desire arises in you that you might want to take one doable step toward?

What might I risk today in service to love?
This is one of those brain-twister questions that may not yield a practical answer; you might want to draw or dance or meditate your way into it.

What loving choices could I make about food this week?
What foods give you energy instead of numbing you? What foods do you eat because they are easy, or fast, or because others in your family like them, even if you don't? When my friend Mary got divorced, she lost fifteen pounds simply because she began to eat exactly what she wanted.

sunday   *monday*   *tuesday*

dates

_____

> *Increasingly accelerate the current of your intuition.*
>
> — Karlheinz Stockhausen

Have to

I want to connect with another amazing human being by:

Choose someone who inspires you. She could be someone you don't know but about whom you want to learn more — or he doesn't even have to be alive! Or think about a new friendship you want to nurture.

One small to-do that has been hanging over my head and making me feel icky is _____. I guesstimate taking care of this would take _____ [amount of time].

Complete this sentence. See if anything shifts in your perceptions. Be realistic — think about how much time the task (or something similar) has taken in the past.

Could do

I'm grateful for:

wednesday   thursday   friday   saturday

Intention:

Let go of

What message have I been sending the universe through my actions, thoughts, words, and moods? Is it in alignment with what I most value, love, and hold dear?
I'm sure it is!

What life insight could help me with any current challenges?
Look back at your list, or perhaps let a trusted friend read your life insight list. Share your current challenges or stresses, and see what ideas you cook up together.

sunday   *monday*   *tuesday*

dates

_____

Have to

What about my actions, choices, and attitudes this year makes me proud?

How can I rest in being enough today?
What would you do if you weren't too afraid or too busy or too unsure if it's Spirit or ego speaking to you? Again, how might your life insights help you?

Could do

I am deserving of:

wednesday   thursday   friday   saturday

Let go of

What gift do I give to the world each day?

You may not know, so guess! Or ask three to five people you trust what they see as your greatest gift, what you can't help but offer to the world.

What could I do to acknowledge my gift?

What would happen if this gift were enough and you didn't have to do anything more?

What is my story about the value of this gift? Does this story make it easier or harder for me to offer my gift?

Do you judge what you easily give as not unique enough? Do you think you aren't good enough to give it? Do you think it's too easy to be of value? And so on.

sunday   *monday*   *tuesday*

dates

_____

Listen with crystal clear clarity to the wild, tender warbling of your desires.

Have to

What do I wish to remember about this gift as I go forward?

How do I wish to share this gift in the near future?

Could do

I wholeheartedly praise myself for:

wednesday   *thursday*   *friday*   *saturday*

Shape of Life Check-in

*T*he following questions and stories are designed to get you back into the flow if you've been "away" from yourself for a while or if you're feeling out of sorts, lost, or befuddled. Or you may find yourself turning to this chapter when you are in some kind of transition, for a reminder that when you connect with yourself, your next step is revealed. Think of these questions and stories as a gentle waterfall beckoning you to stand under it and be refreshed, awakened to all that is good and beautiful and true in you.

- *What small act of kindness could I offer myself in the next hour?*

Laraine, a retreat participant, said it best. "Self-denial is an act of self-hurt, the way it constricts and narrows my life, reinforcing smallness and impoverishment, and cascading out from me negatively to all with whom I interact." Promise yourself some small token of your affection: a foot rub or hand massage with lavender essential oil, ten minutes doing absolutely nothing, talking to someone who thinks you're the cat's meow.

- *How connected am I to my heart these days? When did I last feel connected to myself?*

Address these questions to your heart.

- *What desires want to be heard?*

Don't edit, and let yourself be wild and silly. Let desire speak to you.

Stories for Along the Way: Lain's Paper Scissors Desire

After I had spent two years stealing time from my three young children, sneaking away from my sleeping husband in the middle of the night, and typing a sentence at a time while the laundry wrinkled in the dryer, my first novel was finally done. I spent a few months crossing the t's and dotting the i's and then pronounced that it was time for the next step.

I packed my suitcase and hopped on a plane to attend a popular writers' conference in a distant state. After three days, I had half a dozen agents requesting to read the manuscript, and a well-known editor who wanted to see the book as soon as I had representation. I was in heaven. I sent off all the requested materials, breathed a sigh of relief, and thought, "Now would be a perfect time to start on my next book!"

Then I promptly went to the art store and bought a hundred dollars' worth of supplies.

The next day — and the next, and the next — I tried to convince

> When you feel blocked in allowing guidance or information, ask, "If I didn't know already, what might I notice right now?"

myself that I would be more marketable to agents and publishers if I could get another book under way. I told myself that I could use this downtime to edit the book again, or to look up more agents to send the manuscript to if the current crop didn't pan out. There were a million things, I said to myself, that I *could* and *should* do to keep my writing career going.

I didn't want to do any of them. What I really wanted to do — what I longed to do, what kept me up at night — was to sit at a table in my little walk-in closet that my five-year-old daughter and I call our "craft studio" and get my hands dirty. I wanted to feel paper ripping between my fingers, to smell the unmistakable odor of Elmer's glue. I wanted to dabble in sequins and pigment paints and stamp pads. I wanted to create something full of color and form and fun. I wanted to play. So I did.

I've never been much for playtime. I'm much better at deadlines and to-do lists. So to recognize — and then honor — this longing inside me was startling. And the longing keeps getting bigger and bigger.

Whatever it is, it sometimes feels dangerous, like a tidal wave that might overwhelm me, sweeping me up and then tossing me, spent and broken, on the hard ground. But mostly, it feels energizing — like Dorothy's tornado — carrying me to a new, more colorful place. Whether or not my book gets published, whether or not I write another novel, I am a creative soul, and there are more messages for me to share, and a hundred different ways — and colors — in which to share them.

- *When I've trusted my desires in the past, I have found that...*
You may need to get help with this one by asking someone who knows you well or by looking back at journals or even your date book.

- *What life insights have I been steering my life by lately? What life insights do I wish I'd been using to steer my life?*

One Life Planner user told me that even though she may not recognize it at the time, her life insight list almost always contains the solution to whatever situation she is feeling lost or stuck about.

- *Body, what do you want to tell me about what I need to find my center again?*

Stories for Along the Way:
Nancy Dances in the Kitchen

Before we learned ballroom dancing, my husband used to gather me into his arms in the kitchen, and we would pretend to dance. I never knew what inspired him; I just went along. No music necessary.

Dancing has always been magical for me. When I was four, my mother signed me up for tap lessons. "You could hardly wait to get into those shoes," she says. Black patent leather shoes, with ribbons instead of laces, and metal taps that clicked when I walked. Heaven!

At ten, I wanted to be a ballerina. I adored the dresses and the pink satin toe shoes. Mother purchased a book with photos of elegant dancers, and the book became a dream treasury to study frequently. I loved the graceful arch of the ballerinas' bodies, the delicate lift of their hands. I yearned to move as effortlessly as they did.

As the years passed, my dreams of ballet and tap dimmed as other activities took their places. Yet the desire to express myself through movement never completely dissipated.

Years later, struggling to find myself and not sure that I ever would, I enrolled in a ballet class. At thirty-five, I thought I was honoring a gentle yet insistent longing to dance again. What I didn't know is that I would discover something much more essential.

When I danced, the person I was meant to be became unstuck. This reinforced my determination to move beyond my past and into a new life, one in which self-confidence would supplant fear and in which joy would root out misery. Dancing strengthened my muscles; stretching at the barre forced me to quiet my mind. During the second part of class we danced short combinations to music.

I began to cry whenever we stretched. Deeply held emotions found their way to the surface, and I ached with sadness. After a while, it felt too overwhelming, and I stopped going to class.

What I know now is that the key to unlocking my deepest emotions is dance. And if I continue to move, I can traverse the longing and sadness and arrive at a fresh place, a place of renewed strength and hope. I must dance to find myself.

- *I'm ready to name twenty-five things I am proud of right now, and they are:*

Some of my answers: taking care of my mom, doing the dishes every night, falling in love at forty-five...

- *What do I trust about others and myself right now?*

Maybe it's that the sun will rise, that the dog will lick you, that you like chocolate, that you won't go postal, that you will move your body enough, that you love your parents...

- *What am I trying to know or decide right now that may not be ready to be known or decided?*

Again, look back at what you've been recording. If you haven't been using the Life Planner questions, record what you've been avoiding or meaning to do, and notice what might shift when you declare it isn't quite time for _____.

• *What is the most important gift I have received lately?*
Name what is given.

Stories for Along the Way: Fran's Beige Towels

She handed me two new beige towels that she had bought for me, and I exploded. I spewed a flood of pent-up anger, overwhelm, and humiliation all over my dearest friend and recovery angel.

My friend had arrived the day I came home from the hospital, having cleared her calendar and flown clear across the country to take care of me as I recovered from colon cancer surgery. She slept on the sofa so she could be near me through the night. She cooked, cleaned, did laundry daily, rubbed my back in the middle of the night when the pain was unbearable, changed my bandages and dressed my wound three times a day, bathed me and encouraged me, coached me, loved me, showered me with fresh flowers — fresh flowers in every room of my house! She gave me hope when I felt scared or discouraged. She rented an electronic keyboard and played for me. I was enveloped in an overwhelming expression of unconditional love.

Until she handed me those two new oversized beige towels — then I snapped. I couldn't receive any more love, caring, generosity, or thoughtfulness.

My angel listened while I ranted, and when I had calmed down she said, "Fran, you are heavily shielded. You wear shields to protect yourself from getting hurt, but they also deflect the love that wants to get through to you." I felt the shock of her words as though a powerful floodlight had been turned on me.

That night, lying in bed, I felt the presence of angels. In the comfort of their presence, with my friend within whispering distance in the next room, I began to recognize the lifelong pattern of protective behaviors, played out through my relationships with three abusive husbands. I realized that I had been living my life certain that the world is not safe. I realized with deep sadness all the love I had lost in my life — all the missed opportunities for letting it in. I felt humiliation for all the times that others saw my shields when I could not. I felt angry with myself for withholding my trust in God. I made a decision. I decided that from that moment on I would live my life consistent with a belief that the universe desires only to love me, and that everything I see is an expression of love. I visualized tossing away the shields, and I began feeling a sense of freedom, joy, and a new kind of safety.

I started practicing immediately with the chemotherapy. Even though I was scared of putting it into my body, my spiritual guidance assured me it was important for me to do. So I chose to see the chemo as an expression of the universe loving me. I called it the "love juice." That shift in my perception transformed my fear into openness and trust.

I continue to deepen my capacity to receive love and to expand my ability to see its expression in many forms. Shield free, I am learning to love myself more profoundly, and I am attracting relationships with people who appreciate and nurture who I am.

- *What resources do I need to call on to support my truest life in the coming days and weeks?*

Are you getting more comfortable with being needy and asking for help, from the Source and from others? If not, what might you want to ask for now? Who do you automatically assume can't or won't help you? What do you automatically assume must be done alone?

- *Spirit, Source, God, Nature: What do I need to know about my life right now?*

See what wants to come through you.

- *How can I, in this moment, know that I am okay, no matter what?*

Stories for Along the Way: Dixie on a Horse

On a vacation about ten years ago, I decided to go horseback riding with two friends. I am not a rider, but I thought it sounded like a nice alternative to seeing the area by foot in the heat of the day. I had a slow horse, and everything was very leisurely. However, the area we were riding in was very wooded — dense and wild — and I kept having to lower my head, lean over, or push a branch out of the way. After watching me struggle — although I did not *think* I was struggling — the native guide rode back to me and said in his broken English, "It is better to move the horse, señorita." I remember my shock. I am part of something bigger that was moving. I think of this horseback ride whenever I'm faced with a change or a struggle. Do I lower my head and push away the "branch," or is there another way to move the "horse" and myself away? My horse didn't always want to move, but usually when my intentions were clear and expressed with the right tugs on the reins, we did just fine.

Fruits of the Heart

— ∞ —

*T*hink of this chapter as a tool to help you discern if this way of steering your life is working *according to your standards.* When you live from your heart, you need a way of knowing whether what you are doing is generating the life you want. Far too often, I watch clients (and myself) forgetting to pay attention to *what is actually happening.* Instead we get lost in the noise of what we should be doing, in our fantasies about what we wish was happening, or in our confusion over what others may tell us is the *right thing to do.*

Without a way to assess what we are getting out of our actions, we can waste years on practices and ideas that do not support us in fulfilling and sharing our gifts. We would never do this in business: companies work very hard to assess which efforts yield the best returns. However, businesses also have empirical means of measurement that the heart-shaped path mostly lacks. I can measure an increase in profits; I cannot measure as concretely the increase in my ability to enjoy my life or my ability to love or be of service. That doesn't mean we need to give up on assessing our progress; we just need different tools.

The tools in this chapter are meant to be used after you've been using your Life Planner or otherwise playing with ideas in this book for about three to six months. Or you might find yourself starting the whole process with this chapter because you want to gauge where you are now and appreciate what fruits you are already harvesting — and what things haven't worked too well. Either way, use these ideas to gain perspective and to lovingly help yourself become aware of what your choices are creating.

What Fruits Do You Wish to Bear?

Fruits of the Spirit is a Christian term used in determining if a faith journey is on course. In the New Testament, Paul names the fruits of the Spirit as love, joy, peace, patience, kindness, goodness, gentleness, faithfulness, and self-control. Fruits of the heart are your list, the specific qualities you name and then look for to see if your choices are moving you toward being and feeling and experiencing what is truest for you. They can serve as your mile markers on the spiral road of life. Without them, you can be a like a child in a car at night who believes the moon is following her, or you can fail to see that you have progressed, since you are dealing with the same issue or challenge yet *again*.

- *What fruits of the heart do I hope to see manifest from my current choices and practices?*

Paul wrote his list; what is yours? Paul's is timeless, but your list may change over time as you focus on different needs and desires. For example, a list of my fruits of the heart from several years ago included "greater intimacy with my husband, self-acceptance, regular progress on my novel, and more energy and less of a foggy, ill feeling." My current list: "savoring all of life, following desire, kindness toward myself and others, time for creative joy and as much fun as possible." These are all qualities or actions I can reflect on and even measure to see if I am moving in a direction that feels right and true.

This is not about setting intentions, goals, or practices. Rather, it is about what fruit you are hoping to bear from your day-to-day choices. Form your list by writing about what qualities you want to feel in your life. Then trim your list down to four or five qualities and/or directions. Live with the list for a few days, months, or even years. See what fits. Allow it to change as you notice what is actually bearing fruit, what you are being drawn to, and what matters to you most.

Noticing the Fruit

How do you notice the fruits that are ripening in your life?

You may want to look over your Life Planner pages and recall various life situations and moments, especially stressful ones, and see what has shifted. Are you becoming kinder? More patient? Do you feel more present? More open to your feelings? Do you savor and enjoy your life more often? Are you more inner directed than outer buffeted? Look for your qualities, for what matters to you. It's very simple and very important. Or you might try connecting with your body in a way that relaxes you, then feeling into your heart, finally asking the mindful question, "What is easier or more satisfying to me these days?" or "How true to myself have I been feeling lately?" Stay connected to your heart while you repeat the question until something comes to light. If nothing does, pick up a pen and write for ten minutes without stopping, editing, or hurrying, exploring the same question.

What do you do if you don't like the fruit you're harvesting? You can start by asking yourself:

- *What am I really doing to tend my heart and to bear the fruits I want to taste?*
- *Am I insisting that my heart bear a kiwi when I've planted an apple seed?*
- *By what measurements and in what conditions am I dissatisfied?*

Let's explore these questions in some detail.

What Am I Really Doing?

Being human, we often seem to believe we are doing something (like working with our thinking patterns or exercising daily) when we aren't. Ditto for thinking we have practiced something longer and more diligently than we actually have. This age-old human phenomenon is particularly painful when it comes to attempting to live from your heart; if you believe you have been, for example, taking time to check in with yourself, but you really haven't, you can tell yourself that this life organizing does not work for you, because look at how much you've tried! You then fall back into resignation (thinking "others can have that but I can't") — usually followed by cynicism and bitterness, with a regular dose of shadow comforts. Or you fall into following someone else's idea of what your life should look like or what should matter to you. Either way, you give up.

That's why keeping an account of what you are actually doing to support yourself in living from the inside out can be very useful. It may sound like just one more thing to do or fail at, but it doesn't have to be. The trick is to make whatever tracking system you use part of your Life Planner or calendar, to track only one or two practices at a time, and to be absolutely certain that you are fully and utterly committed to whatever you intend to do.

You might want to keep track of when and how often you:

- Listen for guidance

- Center and ground yourself

- Pause before making a decision to check in with your body and intuition

- Heed something larger than yourself

- Do yoga, practice tai chi, do aikido, dance, sing, make music, write in your journal, make art, walk a labyrinth — in other words, practice an expressive art that feeds you

- Pray

- Meditate

- Offer compassion to yourself and others

- Choose to eat in a way that supports your health and energy

I've tracked writing, doing yoga, meditating, and connecting to God. I've tracked when I've eaten sugar during the day, when I was grateful, when I moved my body. Some examples of what clients have tracked are being creative, painting, not yelling at their children, and billing their patients.

Ways to Keep Track

Keep track by writing, and *do not* make it into a big, hairy deal. I keep track in two ways: by keeping logs and by making notes on my calendar. When it comes to straightforward daily or weekly practices I've committed to, I simply note on my calendar what I did on what day and for how long; it might look like "walked 40" or "yoga 1 hr., writing 30." I never have more than two commitments at a time!

I use logs for practices that tend to get tainted by my wanting or demanding a particular outcome; creative, spiritual, or intuitive endeavors thrive from this added bit of detail. For example, a writing log might look like:

Date	Time	How I Felt	Linkage

How to Use This Log

Date: The point of a log or record is to be able to look back at when and how often you actually did something. Hence, it helps to record the date.

Time: When exactly did you write? Why is this important? You may find you are more productive at certain times. The best times to work can change with age, projects, and even different stages of a project.

How I Felt: Briefly describe what felt good or bad or boring, *not* your feelings about what you wrote. You are looking for inferences that will help you notice if that extra cup of coffee isn't helping, and how mood may affect your output.

Linkage: What will you start with next time? Write down your idea in a word or a sentence.

Do not note anything about the *quality* of your writing.

Other Helpful Log Ideas

Intuition	Fact	Desired Outcome	Actual Outcome

Intuition: What your heart says to do.

Fact: The situation as it actually is.

Desired Outcome: What you think will happen when you do what your heart tells you to do.

Actual Outcome: What actually happened after you took action.

This log will help you ground the tricky job of listening, and over time — and it can take a lot of time — it will help you tease out when you are listening to your ego instead of your heart, when you are focusing on the wrong aspect or question, and when you are focusing on the right one.

Spiritual Practice	How I Felt Before	How I Felt After

Spiritual Practice: Write a few words about what you did: meditated for ten minutes, served the homeless one night, decided it was better to be happy than right and shut my mouth with my partner.

How I Felt Before: A log can show you, in simple facts, that what you feel doesn't have to determine what you do; moods do not have to control you.

How I Felt After: This information can point out how you are being supported, or not, by what you are doing. This is also very valuable information.

Am I Insisting That My Heart Bear a Kiwi When I've Planted an Apple Seed?

You do not order the fruits of your heart from Harry and David. Rather, these fruits spring from your actions; they unfold in their own time and in their own way. We all adore stories about people who listen to their hearts; defy the common; take risks; and are rewarded with fame, lasting love, and spiritual oneness. I've often heard clients equate living from their heart with getting exactly what they want. This is a dangerous misconception. Step away from the magical thinking. It's easy to miss the fruit your heart is bearing if you are comparing your harvest to someone else's, or if you haven't taken the time and effort to see what kinds of seeds you are actually planting. We often recognize this dynamic in young people: if they could accept who they are and stop trying to be someone else, they would begin to taste more of what they want.

Yet how rarely we do this for ourselves. We dismiss what is easy, we shrug off what others find valuable or amazing about us, and we downplay our natural talents. Yet who we are keeps showing up, and one of the benefits of living from our hearts first is the chance to see what we value reflected back to us in who we are becoming. Will you turn away from that reflection because it isn't what you think it should be? What an irony and a terrible waste that would be!

By What Measurements and in What Conditions Am I Dissatisfied?

How many of us set standards that are heart exhausting and mind-numbingly unattainable? When we constantly raise the bar, we feed the condition of wanting to be something we are not. Nothing we do is ever enough. We may say we will be satisfied if we write for ten minutes a day or walk four times a week for thirty minutes, but then we do these things, and the weasel voice in our head whines, "Alice Walker writes for longer than ten minutes" or "You'll never fit into that outfit if you only walk. You need to join a gym and work out really hard for two hours a day!"

If you find yourself dissatisfied with the fruits that are ripening in your life, you must first ask yourself:

• *Why?*

Why isn't it enough? What do you want instead? Who has that? What did he or she do to cultivate these fruits?

- *Whose measurements or conditions am I using?*

Mostly, we don't have any measurements, or if we do, they are vague. Do you want to be happier? Then decide what will satisfy you, recognize it when it shows up, and let yourself rest there, refusing to raise the stakes on yourself or to demand more before you have even appreciated what you have. Relentless dissatisfaction is a form of self-violence, and it damages your ability to listen to your heart — it may even damage your actual heart muscle. This doesn't mean you will necessarily feel satisfied. Your mind will almost always tell you, "More, more!" Stay with your declaration to be satisfied. That's different from *feeling* satisfied. Feelings change as fast as your thoughts. Declarations, however, create an anchor to return and to hold fast to.

- *What will truly satisfy you when it comes to the benefits of living from your heart first?*
- *What fruit do you want to taste?*
- *What seeds are you planting?*

Without declarations of what will satisfy you, without mile markers to check your evolution against, you'll lose focus, momentum, and faith. Put in place ways to assess your passage, for it is only through experience and *noticing those experiences* that you create a life of authentic trust and lived faith instead of magical thinking and half-baked wishes. Experiment with what will ground and anchor your heart-lived life and always, always remember that it is completely human to stumble and forget and utterly predictable that you will do so. When you do (not if), ask yourself the most powerful mindful question of all: *What if it was completely okay to be doing and feeling and being exactly who I am right now?*

What if you didn't need to change a thing?

Hands on Hearts

*T*he first time I finished writing this book was in the waiting room of the Virginia Mason Cancer Institute in Seattle, Washington. I was waiting with my dad, who was receiving treatment for pancreatic cancer. I remember how much fun we had in that waiting room, Mom, Dad, and me. Dad was dying — although he lived for a full two years after his diagnosis — and that made our time together, anywhere, so joyous. Just happy to be together. And still, on the ferry ride across Puget Sound that day, I remember entertaining the thought that if my life as a writer and personal growth teacher were ideal, I would be completing this book in a cabin in the Cascades, immersed in infusing every idea, sentence, and word with love, undisturbed by anything except perhaps the piercing call of a single hawk. I remember being suddenly sure that because I was not, I was a failure and a fraud.

I'm happy to say it took me only about two hours to realize the absurdity of the story I was telling myself. Finishing this book on a day that included my daughter yelling at me because I told her the wrong time for her babysitting job (did not, by the by), the trip to the hospital to hear Dad's cancer was spreading, watching two armed Coast Guard patrol boats accompany the ferry because of terrorist risk, and a friend dropping off a homemade pie, was perfect. This book is made for days like that, and days like this one, the one I am having as I finish the edits for the new edition.

This is a day that I started with meditation and journaling, checking in with myself. Then I ran over to my mom's to make sure she took her pills — she lives alone near us now and has Alzheimer's. Then a spot of wedding planning — I'm getting married for the second time, to my love, Bob — which included trying on my wedding dress to find it's uncomfortably tight, and the wedding is in three weeks! It's also a day of helping my new in-laws move to the island, helping my daughter, home from college, navigate summer job politics, and planning my annual writer's retreat. In other words, another perfect day.

Life organizing helps me accept my life and myself. My deepest wish is that it does the same for you, and that this book reminds you to always treat yourself with kindness, and always, always trust your wise heart.

I hope we meet — online or in person — one day soon. I give great hugs!

Notes

8   "*Transcendence, the ability to rise...*" Joseph Chilton Pearce, *The Biology of Transcendence* (Rochester, VT: Park Street Press, 2002).

19 *Crown Pull...* Donna Eden, *Energy Medicine* (New York: Tarcher, 1999), 77.

20 "*Discoveries in the field of neurocardiology...*" Joseph Chilton Pearce in an interview with Casey Walker, "Waking Up to the Holographic Heart," *Wild Duck Review*, vol. IV no. 2, Spring/Summer 1998, page 28 and following.

24 "*The ability to intentionally shift...*" Marilee G. Adams, *Change Your Questions, Change Your Life: & Powerful Tools for Life and Work* (San Francisco: Berrett-Koehler, 2004), 3.

31 "*very next physical actions required to move...*" David Allen, *Getting Things Done* (New York: Penguin, 2002).

37 "*And now abideth faith, hope, desire...*" Joseph T. Shipley, *The Origins of English Words: A Discursive Dictionary of Indo-European Roots* (Baltimore: Johns Hopkins University Press, 2001).

39 "*those that can enjoy desiring and those...*" Adam Phillips, *Darwin's Worms* (New York: Basic Books, 2001).

39 "*It is possible to be in a state in which desire...*" Mark Epstein, MD, *Open to Desire* (New York: Gotham Books, 2005).

41 "*What would I love to make...*" Michael Neill, *You Can Have What You Want* (London: Hay House, 2006).

53 "*We do not see how things are; we see...*" Alan Sieler, *Coaching and the Human Soul* (Melbourne: Newfield Australia, 2003).

77 "*Comfort did not always have its present 'soft'...*" John Ayto, *The Dictionary of Word Origins* (New York: Little, Brown & Co., 1990).

84 "*We have been trained to think of situations...*" Robert Fritz, *The Path of Least Resistance* (New York: Fawcett Columbine, 1989).

100 "*I have often maintained that...*" Pablo Neruda, "Towards the Splendid City" (Nobel Lecture, Stockholm, December 13, 1971), available at http://nobelprize.org/nobel_prizes/literature/laureates/1971/neruda-lecture-e.html.

Acknowledgments

— ∞ —

*M*y gratitude is unbounded for the infusion of wisdom and often wise and sometimes wacky support that I received while writing this book. Gratitude truly is the mood that opens up my creativity. (Thank you David Martin for that wisdom.)

To the hundreds of women who took the time to send in your stories and frame your life wisdom, especially Elaine Whitesides, Dana Reynolds, Noelle Remington, Jo Hatcher, Amarja Kamp, Melissa Daimler, Karen Ryan, Erin Corcoran, Monica Englander, Shannon Lyn Boyington, Sally Stanton, Andrea Scher, Merri Hiatt, Pixie Campbell, Nancy Barbata, Dixie Mills, Ellen Ziegler, Carla Blazek, Diana Lieffring, Shelby Frago, Marcie Telander, Rhonda Hull, Jennifer Freed, Julie Kearney, Wendy Taylor, Tricia Bath, Suzanne Monson, Karen Ely, Amy Cooper, Janet Lucy, Sara Lou O'Connor, Deanna Chvatal, Fran Fisher, Laraine Armenti, and so many more.

To my mentors and supporters, with special thanks to Julio Olalla, Willow Pearson, Lynn Robinson, Mark Silver, Molly Gordon, Laura Berman Fortgang, Sara Flick, Lainie Ehmann, Victoria Moran, Ann Cheng, Billie Taylor, and Marissa N. Perez.

To my brain trust group for so much — Michele Lisenbury Christensen, Michael Bungay Stanier, Molly Gordon, Mark Silver, and Eric Klein.

To the earlier adopters of the Inner Organizer who dare to live with more awareness, self-kindness, and pluck, especially Poppy Casper, Helga Wocherl, Cindy Landy, Wendy Hennequin, Karen Leary, Diedra Truman, Joan Volkmann, and Zoe Crook.

To Georgia Hughes, my patient and amazingly trusting editor; and to Kristen Cashman, managing editor; Tracy Cunningham, a whiz graphic designer; Tona Pearce Myers, gifted typesetter; Alexander Slagg, amazing master of everything, and publicist Monique Muhlenkamp.

To the gift of synergy in seeing Alicia LaChance's art at Fraga Gallery — I'm so very thankful.

To Stephanie Kip Rostan for outstanding patience, loyalty, and gentle care-taking.

To Debbie Buxton and Amber Kinney, my left-brains — you rock.

To Lillian, heart of my hearts, I am so blessed to call you my daughter.

Finally, to Bob. "Lovers don't just meet somewhere, they're in each other all along." Here's to meeting now and forever.

About the Author

*J*ennifer Louden is a writer and personal growth teacher who helped launch the self-care movement with her first book, *The Woman's Comfort Book*. She's a personal coach, a retreat creator, a speaker, a popular blogger, and the author of five other books on well-being, including *The Woman's Retreat Book*. She lives on Bainbridge Island, Washington, and believes that self-love + world love = wholeness for all. She'd love to gift you a free Life Organizer app, a download-able copy of the weekly questions, and audio love letters — just visit jenniferlouden.com/lifeorganizer.